Finding a Moral Heart for U.S. Immigration Policy: An Anthropological Perspective

Josiah McC. Heyman

American Ethnological Society Monograph Series, Number 7
Mary Moran, Series Editor

Printed in the United States of America
Production editor: John Neikirk
ISBN 0-913167-88-6

Library of Congress Cataloging-in-Publication Data
Heyman, Josiah McC. (Josiah McConnell), 1958-
Finding a moral heart for U.S. immigration policy: an anthropological perspective / Josiah McC. Heyman.
p. cm.—(American Ethnological Society monograph series ; no. 7)
Includes bibliographical references.
ISBN 0-913167-88-6
1. United States—Emigration and immigration—Government policy.
2. United States—Emigration and immigration—Regional disparities. I. Title. II. Series.
JV6483.H48 1998
325.73—dc21
98-27617
CIP

Copies may be ordered from:

American Anthropological Association
4350 North Fairfax Drive, Suite 640
Arlington, VA 22203

Contents

Acknowledgments

Many people have made this monograph possible. My wife Merlyn and I share abiding moral and social concerns; what I have written partakes of this. I particularly thank Mary Moran, who has been a superb editor, and the anonymous referees who commented perceptively on the manuscript. I owe a large debt to the scholars with whom I have had conversations over the years; they may not have realized that I was picking their brains, and they may or may not much like what I have written, but they did help me enormously. In particular, I thank Eric Wolf, Sid Mintz (for a key suggestion at the start), Leo Chavez, Robert Alvarez, Carlos Vélez-Ibañez, Michael Kearney, Juan-Vicente Palerm, Jim Greenberg, Tim Dunn, Kye-Young Park, Kathy Halvorsen, Carol MacLennan, Mary Durfee, and Barry Solomon. I also thank a number of scholars for making available to me working papers and unpublished papers. I thank many interviewees inside and outside the INS who cannot be named. Friends in Agua Prieta, Sonora and Douglas, Arizona continued to teach me about border affairs. Research on the INS and immigration issues at the Mexican border was supported by grants from the Harry Frank Guggenheim Foundation and the Wenner-Gren Foundation for Anthropological Research. Writing of the monograph was supported by a Faculty Development Grant from the Vice-Provost for Research at my university, Sung Lee, and facilitated by my department chair, Terry Reynolds. All responsibility for errors of fact or interpretation remains my own.

Summary of the Immigration Policy Proposal and Its Rationale

At the present, the United States receives extensive immigration, but part of it is covert and illegal; worse, there is little acceptance of migrants, even those who come legally and openly. This situation exacerbates cultural and political conflicts, while eroding toleration and accommodation to change in the nation. We *can* envision a different immigration policy, one that does not undermine its own political foundation. An effective approach addresses the roots of conflict and not just the surface of immigration law. It asks how to encourage moral reciprocity by which immigrants and hosts recognize each other's mutual personhood in the framework of a democratic nation.[1] In this monograph, I argue for "local compacts," political forums for deliberating on regionally appropriate immigration policies. Local compacts would require the involvement of people who are normally bystanders or silent partners in immigration processes; for example, they would require that employers and other immigrant recruiters in the host society take responsibility for movement and settlement costs. Through the process of democratic negotiation, the local compact would make fractured groups, who now view each other in narrow stereotypes, recognize their shared personhood. Compacts would address the core failing of current U.S. immigration policy by enhancing local responsibility and commitment between immigrant and host. Is local negotiation and regionally flexible immigration policy workable and desirable? Could it resolve real conflicts? To add a dimension of realism to the proposal, I review how the local-compact approach might work in actual, highly varied U.S. immigration situations, as documented by anthropologists.

Local compacts would be guided toward success by the discoveries of the social sciences about human migration. The key idea is flexible, self-regulating systems,[2] rather than top-down numerical control. Local compacts would control immigration through recruitment rules, rather than numerical quotas, the present system. We know from current experience that numerical control works poorly, if at all. In contrast, research suggests that influencing how networks recruit persons to migrate would effectively get the word out about when to enter the nation and the locality. A flexible-recruitment migration system would be at least as capable of regulating the total number of U.S. immigrants as the current system, with its failed numerical ceilings and sub-rosa "illegal" entries. The proposal also suggests ways to integrate a national moral commitment to giving asylum into local compacts. One powerful way to influence recruitment networks and to make pro-migration actors (e.g., employers and coethnics) responsible for their choices would be to impose a "compact tax" on migrant recruiters that would pay for local investments in schools, housing, community policing, medical services, and so on. The aim is not only to reshape the choices of immigrants (the usual objective in migration control) but also the choices of the receiving society. The give-and-take of deciding on recruitment, costs, and shared goods would promote the key good: mutual moral commitment between immigrant and host.

In the new policy, the Immigration and Naturalization Service (INS) would facilitate the local-compact negotiations and coordinate the recruited streams of migrants. These new roles would promote a more sophisticated, professional INS. The proposal would also entail a positive role for U.S. borders as key places for regulating immigration transactions, rather than a negative role as zones of illegality and policing. This is consistent with the richer and more complex international and transnational relations the United States is building with its fellow nations. In the aspects recited thus far, present arrangements work poorly, and there is a strong case for change. Because no immigration policy could be perfect in a complex world, however, and because the new approach seeks difficult and contradictory goals, this monograph takes into consideration a number of serious objections and challenges to the proposal, including environmental impacts of migration, U.S. population size, and consumption; the effects of immigration on poor and working-class Americans; cultural change and the evolution of American pluralism; and so on.

There is no guarantee that a drastic change in immigration policy will be supported in the present U.S. political climate. But my proposal merits careful reading nonetheless, for it addresses issues and conditions that narrowly conceived policy debates ignore. It draws attention to changing the immigration debate itself, its atmosphere of moral divisiveness, fear, and hostility. The proposal's awareness of the concerns of hosts and migrants comes from an anthropological perspective. Anthropology, distinctively among all fields, seeks to understand the fundamental human condition, and thus confronts the dilemma at the heart of U.S. immigration struggles: each group in their humanity wields a narrow moral compass, and does not recognize the similar humanity in other persons and groups. The huge size of the modern nation, its segmented and unequal character, and the dynamism of the modern economy simply worsen this human tendency. But anthropology is not gloomy about humanity; it offers us reason to envision stitching together people in constructive, imaginative, and affirmative ways.

Notes

1. As the legal scholar Alexander Aleinikoff (1997) demonstrates, immigration policy is fundamentally about "circles of membership."

2. In emphasizing the virtues of "flexibility," I recognize that I am influenced by the intellectual climate of my time, specifically the use of metaphors of flexibility and complexity in an era of mobile capitalism, as diagnosed by Emily Martin (1994). One concern with flexibility situated in contemporary capitalism is that it justifies elites reneging on their responsibilities to located people and communities. It is clear that my proposals seek very much the opposite: greater local accountability being required of employers, political elites, and so on. I also have good reasons for particularly emphasizing flexibility in that U.S. immigration policy's most pressing flaws come from its inflexibility, despite its relative generosity in terms of numerical admissions. Nevertheless, flexibility is not a cure-all, a magic formula, but rather a means toward a process of moral engagement and mutual decision making. It is only by situating flexibility in this context that we can keep its appeal as a metaphor under control.

Dedicated to Eric R. Wolf,
with the deepest respect

1
Anthropology, Morality, and Immigration: An Overview of the Monograph

I hold that the ways that immigrants and hosts relate to each other politically, socially, and culturally need to change. This monograph includes a schematic policy, but it puts little emphasis on prescriptions that state "in this policy, people will be required to do this thing, and forbidden to do that." Instead, it suggests that immigrants and hosts could develop their own policies in the sense of mutual accommodation. The idea is to affect this through an institutional context that increases cooperation and channels conflict. In this sense, my proposal is unlike what one would expect from a political scientist, economist, or policy specialist whose analysis would be confined to legal forms and existing political conditions. Its anthropological approach has a comprehensive perspective on the human condition, one that attends to the social, economic, political, and cultural contexts enveloping the immediate policy questions. The anthropological perspective opens the more radical range of possibilities explored in this proposal. More importantly, it emphasizes people making their own solutions, expressed through its core inquiry into human moral tendencies synthesized with legal, political, and economic processes in the contemporary United States.

But should anthropology be involved in value-based advocacy at all?[1] As a field, it is often esoteric and rather less often devoted to "issues of the day." Perhaps anthropology is a science whose devotion to learning is compromised by adherence to one side or another in a heated political debate. Furthermore, anthropologists as such do not necessarily agree on value positions. When we cite anthropological findings and analyses, how are we to distinguish between cases that we argue as individuals, dedicated to personal causes, versus those we argue from a coherent disciplinary perspective? The reader should note that in most instances in this monograph, I will use the pronoun *we* to mean anthropologists who are grounded in disciplinary knowledge and who are involved, in one way or another, in policy questions about U.S. immigration, and politicized issues more generally.

These questions are vital to anthropologists because we are drawn, through our encompassing research and expansive worldview, into social critiques and policy positions. We can begin with a recent debate between Roy D'Andrade (1995) and Nancy Scheper-Hughes (1995) which portrays the dilemma facing us, torn between our moral empathy for people and our scientific role. Scheper-Hughes argues that the discipline is inherently value filled because cultural anthropologists morally connect with the people they live among and study. She is most concerned with the morality anthropologists ought to choose (as discussed in the next chapter). D'Andrade, in contrast, doubts that anthropology ought to make moral engagements at all. He is particularly concerned that the moralizing style of writing critical of the status quo prevents the free play of scientific disproof. Although he does not openly state this, it is fair to say that D'Andrade does implicitly hold a value, specifically, knowledge for its own sake. As Roy Rappaport (1995:243–244) shows, the scientific impulse in anthropology rests on this distinctive value choice. The commentators who followed the D'Andrade/Scheper-Hughes debate in *Current Anthropology* generally held that the scientific and political-moral impulses in anthropology were not mutually exclusive, so that effective science could be done on morally chosen topics. I agree, but this "a bit of both sides" approach does not resolve the hard questions and real disagreements exposed in the debate. Can we move beyond polarized positions? How? To answer, it is helpful to cluster the disagreements and unresolved issues in two sets of questions. First, what values ought anthropologists share? How do we relate values such as human empathy and the disinterested search for knowledge? Second, what moral actions do we find in the actual practice of current anthropology? Are there potentially useful, undeveloped moral practices? How does moral practice affect the disciplinary quality of anthropology? The next chapter will consider these questions at length, though I can hardly promise definitive answers.

I do have a position, however. Our values are not idiosyncratic; rather, they come from the knowledge and practice of anthropology. We also have personal and political concerns, but when we undertake an anthropological role and its body of knowledge, perforce we adopt anthropological values. The philosopher Virginia Held (1984) argues persuasively that in well-defined "roles" people *do* share values, and furthermore that such value-imbued roles justify social action. I propose that as anthropologists we share the following propositions: prior to being divided into social groups, people share common humanity; as human beings, moral behavior starts with the recognition of mutual personhood; when people recognize this, their highly personalized interchange of opinions about each other results in effective mutual moral regulation. When people do not recognize their mutual personhood, they can do horrendously immoral acts to each other. The positive side of this moral analysis thus does not always happen, but our ability to state it offers a potentiality, a process whose ideal end point is greatest possible use of this human moral tendency. Our moral role as anthropologists is learning more about such interchange in a disinterested way *and* advocating social arrangements that increase such moral exchange.

I will later review the many ways that anthropologists can and do act on this knowledge. I emphasize a specific practice, however: constructive writing. Constructive writing presents a fundamental vision of what good society and culture might look like. It alternates between explicit value choices (what ought to be) and extensive disciplinary learning (how people actually do relate to each other). In that sense, it is speculative but grounded. Constructive writing contrasts with deconstructive and critical writing that knows what it is against, but not what it is for—that is, writing that is less explicit about value choices and the means to a better society. Constructive writing fits anthropology in one additional way. In doing it well, we acknowledge the challenges of conflict, complexity, process, and scale; we rely on the rich fieldwork of anthropologists to keep an equilibrium between realism and vision.

This monograph can be read by two audiences: for anthropologists generally, this chapter and the next discuss controversies and practices of engaged anthropology; for persons interested in immigration issues, the remainder of the monograph discusses my policy proposals. I hope, however, that the reader can be persuaded of the unity of both themes. Constructive writing explains why I envision in detail a new U.S. immigration system and do not just critique the existing one, while my anthropological interest in human propensities to moral action justifies the fundamental policy approach, including the local-compact system. The anthropology thus informs the policy proposal. Conversely, the immigration case study demonstrates how constructive writing can be done in an intellectually rigorous fashion. Because of this interplay, it is helpful to review the sequence of my arguments.

In the chapter that follows, "Values and Anthropology," I ask "what is a distinctly anthropological perspective on policy controversies?" "what do anthropologists value?" and "what are some realistic moral practices for the field of anthropology?" At the end of that chapter, when I present constructive writing, I point out that the problem of visionary anthropology is not its idealism per se but the need to integrate with it a complex, rather critical view of the world—for example, to address inequality, segmentation, and conflict. The next chapter, "Foundational Values and Real World Challenges," uses the work of Roy Rappaport and Eric Wolf to explore the reconciliation of idealism and critical realism. I take the core of that problem to be how constructively to span immediate, interpersonal moralities and national and global processes. Together with the conclusion, these first two chapters contain my general anthropological arguments.

The remainder of the monograph extends these ideas through a radical reconstruction of U.S. immigration policy. The history and analysis of immigration policy can be daunting for readers not already immersed in the field. The chapter "Recent Immigration to the United States" surveys the basics. It starts by reviewing the history, laws, and conventional debates of U.S. immigration policy. Interestingly, current disagreements about immigration policy (e.g., should migrants receive public benefits) express deeper disorders and discontents. I identify two such disorders as central to immigration policy: the moral disconnection between immigrants and hosts, resulting in *anti-immigrationism*, and the *failure of numerical control* as a regulatory mechanism. Much of the pressure for strict numerical control comes from anti-immigrationism, so I offer an extended theoretical and empirical analysis in the chapter of the same name.

Having started with a critique of immigration policy, the monograph then shifts to constructive proposals. In the chapter entitled "The Basic Plan: Recruitment and the Receiving Situation," I address the failure of numerical control by calling for the legalization of flexible recruitment networks. I outline how a recruitment approach could work, using actual U.S. immigration ethnographies. In this chapter, I address much of the "nitty-gritty" of immigration policy by proposing revision of important legal aspects of migration, including national origins, family and occupational preferences, permanence of residential status, visa numbers, and so on. In the chapter that follows, "Local Compacts: Basic Format, Process, and Examples," I continue the major policy outline, in this instance emphasizing arrangements for democratic political participation and conflict resolution in immigration. Again, this chapter uses actual ethnographies of immigration politics in the United States in order to address forthrightly the possibilities and difficulties of moral interchange between immigrants and hosts in a democratic nation. The chapter on local compacts also discusses the taxation of immigrant recruiters to provide for local and regional services, a critical part of the proposal. That chapter closes with a brief addendum on refugee policy in the new immigration system.

The heart of the monograph is complete at this point but important, albeit secondary, topics await. The chapter "Long Term Settlement under Local Compacts" argues against the idea that immigrant types (cultures, races, educational levels, etc.) are immutable and will fissure U.S. society. Anthropological studies of contemporary U.S. immigrants emphasize how the context of permanent settlement shapes immigrant futures; I suggest that the moral center of compact politics would be the local setting of settlement. The next chapter examines borders, especially with Mexico. Can a relaxed immigration system have realistic control over borders? Actual observations of the U.S.-Mexico border give lie to the assumptions behind that question. I argue that the current approach undermines both legal control and humane development on U.S. borders by making smuggling profitable, while the alternative policy would provide realistic possibilities for border control. The chapter that follows looks at the administration and enforcement of the new immigration policy under a professionalized and strengthened Immigration and Naturalization Service (INS). To explain why and how the INS would change, I analyze the present INS, including my ethnographic observations on the work process of INS officers. In "Foreign Relations," the last of this set of supplementary chapters, I consider the international context of U.S. immigration reform. Because the decisions to migrate are global, not national, this section addresses how a flexible entry system can self-regulate the massive numbers of possible migrants.

In the penultimate chapter, I address major challenges and objections to the immigration proposal. These include the unlikeliness of legislating a radical immigration alternative in the present U.S. political climate; the possibility that if local compacts were used, they would be "captured" by powerful interests, such as employers; the concern that open immigration would injure poor blacks and Latinos; and finally the environmental effects of immigration, including population and consumption increases in the United States. To anticipate my position in that last debate, I suggest that moral regulation and participation in migration policy is a first step toward public participation in decisions of overall "scale," the fundamental issue in ecological politics.

I conclude the monograph by returning to my beginning, assessing the uses and challenges of positive writing in moral anthropology. Immigration conflict, because it is not prone to superficial sympathies and easy critiques, is fertile ground in which to nurture our moral thinking and practice. I hope that my readers will agree: anthropologists *can* envision a world in which we are more fully human, and humane.

Notes

1. The reader should know that for the sake of liveliness and variation in writing, I have used three phrases for moral value-based anthropology: engaged anthropology, value-based anthropology, and advocacy anthropology. The three phrases are not identical, of course, but for our purposes they can be taken as synonymous; I try to be more specific about important distinctions when I survey moral practice in anthropology.

2
Values, Activism, and Anthropology

As exemplified in the D'Andrade/Scheper-Hughes debate cited above, anthropology is riven with disagreement over social activism and moral values. The issues can be divided into two inquiries asking "what does anthropology value?" and "what actual moral practices does anthropology engage in?"

Value Choices

What values, if any, do anthropologists share? That question might put off some readers who would argue that values are personal and variable. I reply that we do gravitate, imperfectly, to an intellectual tradition (or several intersecting traditions) when we become anthropologists. For example, most anthropologists recognize the disciplinary subject matter to be human beings, rather than specific, reified ethnic traditions. Our field is not English literature, or Japanese history, but anthropology. Implicitly, we accept the common humanity of different peoples, times, and places. As I argued above, this distinctive intellectual practice encumbers us with an obligatory "role morality." Roy Rappaport (1995:243–257), for example, shows that scientific anthropology developed in Boasian antiracism as a bearer of and contributor to ideals of "common-humanity." We *should* speak out when our perspective is relevant to issues of public concern. The difficulty, as seen in the D'Andrade/Scheper-Hughes debate, is balancing two values: knowledge for its own sake and our knowledge about common humanity, both of which arise in our role as anthropologists.

I see complexity there, but not a contradiction. Our knowledge does not stand apart from us; it motivates us to moral action. Knowledge is contingent and accumulative, admittedly, so that what might seem a clear role value at one time may change in the future. Accepting this precaution, let me delineate a generalization about morality that many anthropologists share. What is common to human moralities? Surely not specific rules; cross-cultural differences are too great. Instead, we find commonality in the moral patterns embedded in the human species's nature.[1] Mary Midgely (1991), looking at the evolution of morality, proposes that humans emerged with a powerful capacity to engage each other in direct, rich relationships. There is much choice in the content of these relationships, but choices are premised on acknowledging mutuality in the relationship. Frans De Waal (1996) likewise suggests that morality comes from the evolved capacity for empathy with specific individuals. The moral emphasis in these accounts is not on altruism per se, but rather on the recognition that another person is indeed a person and not a disposable object. Donald Brown's cross-cultural characterization of the "universal people" states that "reciprocity . . . is a key element in their morality. So, too, is their ability to empathize" (1991:139). George Silberbauer's (1991) trenchant essay on ethics in small-scale societies shows surprising (to conventional abstract, rule-bound morality) but very effective features of human moral regulation. Rules are broken and transgressions ignored, but moral order remains strong because of resilient webs of observation, commentary, criticism, expectation, obligation, reciprocity, and so forth. In summary, we find two patterns, mutual personhood and flexible, face-to-face regulation.

Human morality is not the opposite of conflict and mistreatment; the horrendous capacity to vilify and victimize persons thought of as "others" or "opposites" comes directly from noninclusion in a morality based on inclusion. For example, Brown generalizes that the "universal people" have a strong in-group/out-group division. In this regard, W. Penn Handwerker (1997) offers a more sophisticated reading of the biosocial bases of human morality. He suggests that people have underlying mental architectures for recognizing violence and freedom from violence (a specific moral sense, that is). Such "meanings" are not limited to cultural groups so much as they are stimulated and applied through social interactions, which usually are local but are not "bounded" to any one group.[2] Robin Fox (1989), who argues forcefully for a biosocial concept of evolved morality, makes a pessimistic reading of this material: people in the world today operate with issues and at scales (e.g., mass international migration) that our ancestors did not face in their adaptive context. This legacy thus does not suffice in the present; it may even worsen our dilemmas. Fox is persuasive about the adaptive lag in biosocial morality, but I depart from his perspective in seeing our species tendencies as the way to address contemporary issues in an optimistic ("constructive") rather than pessimistic voice. Thus, I envision an anthropological moral role in advocating societal arrangements that stimulate the human moral sense and increase the recognition of mutual personhood across social boundaries. In a more critical vein, I urge that we diagnose contexts and ideologies that weaken, restrict, or distort mutual personhood. Either way, pessimists and optimists would agree that relational meanings and mutual regulation are *the* effective domains for *doing* human morality.

Many readers will object to a bold assertion about human nature. This merits extended debate, but not here. Let us, however, briefly consider the charge of biological reductionism; in this matter, I find persuasive Midgely's (1994) position that an evolutionary perspective on human morality reveals dynamism and choice in human species's nature, by contrast with reductionisms and determinisms. Human ethics is a process with contradictory end points, thus one imbued with significant choices for how we make and remake societies. The relational ideal thus does not offer a utopia based on a master principle; rather, it makes us more aware of our choices and their consequences. I ask that readers bear with my generalization long enough to see it played out in a substantial case: migration to the United States. While persuasiveness in a particular case does not prove universality, it does suggest whether it is "good to think," or altogether vaporous and wishful.

Promoting mutual recognition of moral personhood is not the only value stance available to anthropologists.[3] Cultural relativism is probably the *moral* stance most widely expressed by cultural anthropologists (though perhaps less in the other subfields). By this I mean the ideas that moral action is relative to local meanings and practices, and that the role of the anthropologist is explaining, defending, and positively evaluating all local cultural moralities. Scheper-Hughes (1992) provides a powerful critique of cultural relativism as a moral stance. "Moral" practices she observed in northeastern Brazil, such as mothers withdrawing care from weak children and doctors medicating away the pain of hunger and stress, are not just local meanings; their contexts include regional, national, and even global political economy. In a parallel critique of relativism, Alain Finkielkraut (1995) urges us to abandon culture and other collective moral concepts in favor of viewing each person as an isolated individual with liberal rights. He particularly fears the connections of group moral relativism to nationalism and group persecution. As appealing as this is for debating against nationalism and in favor of human rights, it is not a realistic model of human moral life, not one that makes much sense for anthropology as a science.

Scheper-Hughes (1992, 1995) grapples more effectively than Finkielkraut with the relativism problem. She offers in replacement a moral anthropology based on the relationship of person (anthropologist) with person; this implies a moral condemnation of societies and cultures that damage the humanity of people the anthropologist knows. This is consistent with the idea of mutual moral regulation, since it reflects the bonds developed between ethnographer and hosts. The ethnographer's experience, however, is not an adequate foundation on which to build a moral practice for the entire field of anthropology. It heightens self-importance on the part of the ethnographer, overvaluing personal proclamations of morality. Also, it depends too much on the individual encounter. Let me refer briefly to my field and analytical experiences. First, it mattered with whom I related, with the frightened undocumented Mexican boy crossing the Otay mountains, or the Border Patrol agent in charge of the Brown Field Station, bemoaning organizational politics that impede easy arrests. Obviously, I empathized cognitively with INS officers in order to study their work life, but that could not be the moral basis for my policy positions. Second, in the vast social field of immigration, no one ethnographer has complete personal contact or knowledge. Instead, my ability to make moral arguments rests on what I learn from the network of fellow scholars. It presupposes, and speaks to, a scientific practice. Therefore, as I write, I channel my personal moral response into intersubjective communication. Third, I am less concerned with my moral recognition of immigrants as persons than I am with U.S. citizens' recognition of the same. This implies less emphasis on direct action with people in the field, which depends on my personal presence, and more emphasis on struggling for a good society that facilitates immigrants and hosts enacting moral exchange themselves.

Mutual personhood, however, cannot be the only value in the anthropological constellation. We recognize human moral patterns by means of another value: knowledge for its own sake. This value is an ideal that anthropology should not abandon. Our living ability to discuss moral questions, both human first-principles and empirical situations, depends on the health of disciplinary anthropology. If we are humble, we will admit that our naturalistic moral conclusions are tentative and can change, and thus that we continue to learn. "Knowledge for its own sake" does need to be checked in one way, by restricting the misuse of people to gain information (e.g., it limits inquiry into restricted ritual knowledge), and recognition of mutual personhood between host and anthropologist should help in this instance. The conjunction of two value stances in our field makes doubly valuable participatory research (knowledge for the sake of people and researcher [Uphoff 1996]). The difficult issue is whether moral anthropology and anthropology for its own sake are compatible in the long run.

D'Andrade (1995) suggests that they are not. He is most concerned with the introduction of value biases into specific inquiries. This is a particularly helpful critique for engaged (advocate) anthropologists. Our work must strive toward the ideal of intersubjective communication about the sensed world, testing, and replication that are at the core of the scientific process. D'Andrade is correct that politics tempts us to bend these strictures, and thus his caution is well-taken. Inside a community of anthropologists, however, it is possible to become "disciplined" to respect such ideals (by professional socialization, by mutual critique, etc.). In this sense, engaged anthropology is a difficult but not prohibited form of scientific inquiry. D'Andrade moves on, however, to argue that moral anthropology is inherently flawed as inquiry into the world because it simply cannot escape the distortion of cognition by agendas. His alternative is that "the first priority will be to understand how things work" (1995:408). This is a fundamental exclusionary claim: knowledge for its own sake is better as a system for choosing topics than involvement in moral and political debate in the world. Several replies come to mind.

First, the possible directions in understanding how things work are almost infinite, yet we do settle into a few paths. Value-choice agendas (e.g., funded HIV/AIDs research) overtly drive some directions, while others are driven by subtle agendas in the climate of the era or the internal permutations of science. It is naive to think that knowledge-for-its-own-sake anthropology does not reflect the predominant world-views and preoccupations of an era. (See Eric Wolf's [1974a, 1974b] seminal analyses of American anthropology and American society.) Yet rooted inquiries do produce knowledge about the world (as do critiques of their biases and limitations). So why not accept them? Second, we *should not* say that anthropology has one starting point, even something as compelling as "understanding how the world works." Anthropologists wield several interacting values that add to and check each other at different times. For example, in this monograph I start with a value choice that immigrants, especially undocumented immigrants, are human beings. (I recognize their personhood.) I then argue, in a scientifically communicative way, that the present U.S. immigration system causes nonrecognition of their personhood, leading to specific harms, including hundreds of accidental deaths incurred while crossing the border (Bailey et al. 1996; see ch. 5). In proposing an alternative immigration system, I work from an explicit moral stance, but as a result I contrast this ideal approach and the actual immigration system. These contrasts, I suggest, advance our understanding of the world as it is—they make us see the symbolism and political economy of U.S. migration more clearly, analytically, and empirically—although this is ultimately for the readers to decide.

As anthropologists, we ought to seek outcomes rather than delimit exclusive starting points (see Bowlin and Stromber 1997). The simultaneous outcomes of *understanding* and *acting* on the world happen because in our discipline science and human morality are inevitably conjoined by our acceptance of a scientific approach to a human subject matter. Our moral values *connect* to knowledge building, rather than opposing it. Engaged and disengaged anthropology differ, and may clash at times, but they are mutually supportive in the long run.

Moral Practices

The discussion of what values anthropologists hold becomes more realistic when we look at the moral actions anthropologists actually take. The survey I offer here is meant to develop analytical understanding, and is hardly comprehensive. It is helpful to start by distinguishing between *direct* action (as Scheper-Hughes advocates) and *indirectly* intervening through writing, bureaucratic work, and so on. Local participatory research obviously spans both; below, I consider aspects most related to political change in the first segment, and planning, advice, research results, and so on in the second.

Direct involvement appears compelling and romantic, but it is shaped and limited by the ways in which radical social change occurs. For example, in movements of the poor and powerless, two successful patterns, often in combination, lead to fundamental social change: appeal to a moral community, and disruption that scares powerholders into concessions or collapse (among many examples, see Fox 1995; Garrow 1988; Piven and Cloward 1977; Wolf 1969). Thus two forms of effective direct action are moral witnessing and involvement in disruptive popular movements. The latter is particularly tricky. We often hold values and desires for change in a particular issue when there is little or no real prospect that a disruptive social movement is ready to explode. Effective direct intervention is not always available to us.[4] It is also possible in disruptive times that some effective direct actions transgress other moral ideals—necklacing informers with burning rubber tires, for instance (Kuper 1995). If our direct involvement does not occur during a disruptive period, we might consider it a valuable form of participatory research, but we must make our self-presentation as effective radicals and moral activists considerably more humble.

Moral witnessing is another option. The word *witnessing* has cachet among academics, but its social preconditions need to be examined. First, it depends on a community of moral appeal. Dr. Martin Luther King and the Southern Christian Leadership Conference (Garrow 1988) acted deliberately and with great perspicacity to reveal the inequity of segregation through televised police repression of nonviolent protest.[5]. The witness of the civil rights movement was effective because black leaders had developed moral empathy in the national community through many years of struggle, making receipt of witnessed meanings possible. The moral framework must be partly shared (translated) from the sufferers to a wider, actionable political community. It does not exist just because the ethnographer shares the grievances of a local population. Second, effective moral witness requires uncovering, documenting, and defending information in intersubjective communication, providing an aura of open, honest, even naive factuality. Think of the simple documentary style of reports by Amnesty International, International Working Group for Indigenous Affairs, Human Rights Watch, and so on; a fine example in the anthropology of immigration is Nagengast, Stavenhagen, and Kearney (1992). Anthropology as a naturalistic discipline is well equipped for moral witness of the documentary style. Writing in outrage may not be as effective a form of moral witness, though outrage is an important initial motivation.

If the paths to direct involvement in other people's radical change are few, we ought to consider moral action within the university, the society many of us inhabit (Scheper-Hughes 1992:25). This is particularly salient given that American universities are critical suppliers of the professional-technical labor force for big capital and big government. Even teachers of general education courses participate in that production process. But the paucity of reportage about teaching and creative institutional service reveals how little anthropologists (and other academics) value this form of engagement. Perusing the *Anthropology Newsletter* shows more theoretical debates and research networking than such university topics. We should discuss the moral quandaries and constructive agendas of academic workers (see Basch et al. n.d.; Kottak et al. 1997).

Let us now turn to indirect forms of action. Again, it helps to start with a rough distinction, in this case between applied anthropology and engaged academic writing. A useful way to distinguish them is by their funding sources and concomitant engagements with powerholders. Scholastic anthropology is mostly funded by a small set of foundations whose aims are the reproduction of academics (e.g., National Science Foundation) or the strategic visions of elites (e.g., The Ford Foundation). These particular social relations of production allow considerable openness to academic production. (All too often, the purity of tone of moralizing academic anthropology blindly assumes funding sources.) Applied anthropology, by contrast, is mostly funded through heavily negotiated relationships with bureaucrats seeking immediate ends. Applied anthropologists know well the manifold difficulties of retaining values and knowledge claims when struggling with funders (Van Willigen 1993). Why does funding make a difference? What is said and to whom is vital to indirect moral action; the moralizing academic and the applied anthropologist hold in common that they try to persuade another person or audience to act in such and such a way. Thus, each type of support, and the cultural worlds that envelop it, shapes a possible range of moral action.

Turning to applied work first, these anthropologists accept some existing "arena" because of their engagements with funders, powerholders, and participants from below. By "arena," I follow the classic anthropological usage, denoting the available contests, constituencies, resources, and language (Swartz et al. 1966). This provides a gain in moral efficacy, but it sacrifices reconceptualizing the arena itself, the basic debates and distributions of resources.[6] As inherently compromised as applied anthropology may be, however, we cannot dismiss it; a penetrating analysis that does not affect the world holds scant advantage over a compromised but effective analysis and action. Of course, there is participatory applied anthropology funded by, answerable to, and made possible from below (e.g., Stull and Schensul 1987). Such work is tremendously important for applied anthropology, especially if we value people's own moral control projected onto the anthropologist. We are fooling ourselves, however, if we see participatory research as less negotiated than applied anthropology in general; both speak, in words, actions, and documents, to a definite arena, with active listeners and decision makers, be they indigenous activists or bank-loan executives.

An even-handed way to distinguish between applied anthropology and engaged academic anthropology is to ask "how does each define and address the units of responsible moral action?" Given the current dominance of nation-states as units of collective action, their arenas capture much applied writing (even participatory research that works with communities facing policy or legal issues). Other units (e.g., the World Bank) are bureaucracies modeled on, and deeply interpenetrated with, nation-states. Certain of our writings should explicitly recognize status-quo actors and arenas, precisely to insist on the moral *responsibility* that comes along with their power and conscious discretion; for example, if oilfield development will damage a particular indigenous population, then we recommend that actors such as oil companies, banks, host-country governments, indigenous associations, and so on act in such and such ways—the characteristic rhetoric of the applied anthropologist. On the other hand, the sheltered academic arena allows persuasive speech about root causes and assumptions of capitalist development, cultural self-determination, and so on: an indirect form of moral action that is often difficult for applied anthropologists.

Let us pause briefly at this distinction between amelioration and diagnosis of root causes (to wit, the origin of the word *radical* being to "grasp by the roots"). For example, Robert Carlson (1996) has been deeply involved in applied anthropology on AIDS. He also offers a radical analysis of HIV transmission. Confronting the persistence of the exchange of sex for drugs despite knowledge about AIDS, he proposes that certain capitalist category errors (i.e., that commodities bring interpersonal power) are the root cause. This analysis indicates the limits of amelioration, but what actionable arena can cause change in deep capitalist epistemological assumptions? Neither amelioration nor radical analysis is obviously superior as moral action in the world.[7] Instead, their moral power is greater in combination, since changes at the root of things may make ameliorative measures more possible and efficacious. Applied anthropologists ought to state more often the radical preconditions of their problems, and grand critics ought to be more forthcoming with concrete recommendations, thereby confronting challenges and complications. Understanding the strengths and limitations of root-cause analysis puts critical academic writing in perspective.

Most of the controversy over moralizing in anthropology (e.g., the D'Andrade/Scheper-Hughes debate) concerns academic writing that criticizes not only the empirical conditions of life in some place and time, but also models, assumptions, and language in the social sciences. This emphasis brought D'Andrade and Scheper-Hughes to focus on intellectual struggles within the discipline. Perhaps a different angle will be refreshing—how does critical academic writing fare as a public moral practice? Academic writing implicitly suggests moral action to its audience: the readers, often part of the educational system, are assumed to be affected in their analyses, vocabularies, and empirical knowledge. Social science writing is notoriously ineffective at influencing public decisions, except when writers offer convenient rationales for positions that politicians have already chosen. As Nico Stehr (1996) writes, however, overt ineffectuality disguises the impact of ideas and labels on political debates—not a profound role, but not completely hopeless, either. Given that possible impact, academic writing *can* be morally meaningful action, although much academic writing may instead follow the value of knowledge for its own sake. Academic writing addresses the public process in three ways, which often overlap. Negative (or "critical") writing deconstructs the existing system of practices, their root causes, and inferred value priorities. Constructive writing elaborates alternative social patterns based on affirmative value choices at the level of root causes. Finally, policy writing accepts existing arenas, problem definitions, and distributions of resources; as an academic genre, it shares much with the applied work just discussed above, so I shall elaborate on it no further.

Exposure, above all, characterizes negative writing. If we imagine surface exposure as "exposé," then negative academic writing advances to reveal the deep roots of morally repugnant surface traits, thereby indicting an extensive social order. Four features then follow, in varied amounts. Empirical description akin to moral witnessing occurs, but the audience for academic products is not as wide or as predisposed for active response as in classic moral witnessing. Inferred causes or hidden connections are emphasized. Persuasive inference relies on historically developed intersubjective communication, so negative writing rests on a broader discipline. Finally, some authors overturn the language used to describe social and cultural phenomena, seeking to rework the assumptions and categories used in political debates. Deliberately reworking language is valuable, given the impact of social science terminology on public debate. Representation approaches to moral action, however, are potentially self-involving, the writer's sense of moral worth coming from her or his words; they lend themselves to a smug sanctimony, a sense that proper language is a good deed. Language should be of concern, as our work is communicative, but we should also convey an outward-directed sense that moral responsibilities pertain to specific actors, and not just ideas.[8]

Negative writing's main flaw is that, in moving directly to critique, it fails to articulate fundamental assumptions about values. When criticizing, it is easy to assume that readers will all recognize the same ideas about "what is wrong" and, implicitly, what a better social order would look like. In this regard, D'Andrade (1995:407) challenges critics to present a theory of "good power"; his point is usefully provocative. Criticism cannot exist alone. Negative evaluations and even the perception of facts emerge in a gestalt together with background assumptions about positive values. For example, Scheper-Hughes (1992) locates maternal acquiescence in child suffering and death against a background assumption that less-constrained mothers express maternal love and bonding. Likewise, the negative ideas of political oppression and economic exploitation, in fact our whole conceptual apparatus about power and inequality, emerge through modern background assumptions of individuality, equality, democracy, and self-realization (Dumont 1977, 1986). D'Andrade fires off the jibe about good power critically, since he seeks a retreat to ideal "science," but good power is as much a jumping-off point as a retreat. Alternating between anthropology as science and as value set, acknowledging the background ideals pervading modern academia, we can explore affirmative values and possible social orders that might embody them.

Constructive writing has the following qualities. First, it articulates foundational values and states possible means to increase such values in a given social domain. It openly faces what is contingently known about social processes. It recognizes the hardest challenges to the positive vision, so that such work is serious anthropology and not just a mechanical utopia. Second, it uses explicit ideals as counterfactual propositions to illuminate (and sometimes to criticize) hidden patterns in the actual world (Lukes 1974). Third, being academic, it is persuasive analytical writing meant to influence the general tenor of public debate. Although it contains specific recommendations, these are not constrained by likelihood of acceptance in existing power arenas, languages, and so on. The recommendations are rhetorical devices, but not the less helpful and thought-provoking for that. Thus, fourth, such constructive writing differs from applied anthropology by addressing root causes and fundamental designs, rather than ameliorative tactics.

We ought to offer both our critical and constructive academic writings with considerable humility. They are but one expression of rightful moral choice available to anthropologists, and not always the most meaningful ones. Nevertheless, anthropologists possess an unmatched, if flawed and incomplete, perspective on the potentials of the human species, the vast range of human designs for living, and the human capacity for changing situations that appear irremediable. Within this worldview of the discipline, academic writing offers a distinctly expansive and unconstrained voice. A critical but positive vision is the fullest statement of what we share, in science and in morality, through our commitment to anthropology.

Notes

1. Readers with a background in philosophy will recognize that I have sided with the naturalistic approach to morality. In naturalism, values come from an origin outside our cogitations. This is not a uniformly shared assumption, of course. I come to a naturalistic position because of my grounding in anthropology; I see its recognition as part of our "role," as explained in the text. The classic objection is that naturalism embodies a "naturalistic fallacy." Statements of description cannot impel moral action; an "ought" term must enter the statement (given condition X, by my values we ought to do Y, not just because of condition X we do Y). As Charles Pigden (1991) argues, this is a persuasive statement about the grammar of moral sentences but not necessarily a refutation of moral naturalism. Suppose, as in the arguments I will make, that humans best relate with each other under conditions where low-scale mutual moral regulation takes place. We ought (here is that word) to redesign society to optimize that naturally given best condition.

2. The ideal of mutual moral regulation fits with the feminist strain in philosophy that emphasizes relationships and how people learn to act morally rather than asocial rules for what is and is not moral (see Frazer et al. 1992).

3. I restrict the consideration of alternatives to those currently debated among anthropologists. There are, of course, a wider range of options offered in philosophical ethics. Many moral philosophies in the modern era rely on the idea that a moral system can be developed through logical rigor and consistency. This characterizes both utilitarian and Kantian approaches, which otherwise differ. From anthropology, we know that human moral systems are not logically consistent, though they are socially patterned. After one acknowledges the distinctive characteristics of human moral practice, we can use classic philosophical

approaches to clarify our thinking in very helpful ways. There is another tradition in philosophy (e.g., David Hume) that emphasizes moral motivations, such as sympathy and social esteem. This is unquestioningly more realistic. Sometimes, however, this is merged with the idea that ethics are purely subjective or more broadly nonnatural. Obviously, I disagree for humans on the whole (see note 1 for my discussion of naturalism and antinaturalism). One characteristic response to subjectivity in ethics is to seek only logical rigor about such subjective statements, whereas I see less rigor and more objectivity to moral sentiments. Two final philosophical approaches also inform my approach to morality: feminist ethics and virtue ethics. Both of these approaches are helpful because they emphasize moral practice rather than moral logic. (Some virtue ethics is more concerned with the cultivation of the individual than the context that helps or hinders people in interaction, however.) Feminist ethics is discussed in note 2.

4. To show how circumstances of social movements and social disruption facilitate academic activism, the teach-in movement during the American protests against the Vietnam war was situationally possible and proved efficacious.

5. The Southern Christian Leadership Conference (during the civil rights movement) understood the profound witness provided in brutal Birmingham versus the less overtly repressive Albany, Georgia (Garrow 1988:227).

6. Our relationship to people, to long history, and to alternative models of society and culture lead most anthropologists at times to question at least some aspects of the status quo; institutionalized policy writing, pervasive in political science, economics, and other disciplines accepts more unquestioningly the existing arenas. Often, policy experts who have forgotten what lies outside their arena become mere technicians of power. This shows the moral peril of too complete a movement in that direction.

7. We tend to assume that the analytical power of root-cause approaches means that the author has also taken the higher moral road. However, if the ameliorative approach has a reasonable chance of affecting society, while the roots-cause approach remains at the level of reading and writing, then amelioration is a morally stronger option. There is no easy resolution of this balance; rather, both of them are moral roles that we should undertake.

8. Let us note Scheper-Hughes's call to turn from critiques of ethnography to radical "good enough" ethnography, her outstanding documentation and inference about hunger in northeastern Brazil (1992). Likewise, let us note D'Andrade's summary and critique of the model of oppression by concepts rather than economic, political, and cultural relations. D'Andrade is persuasive when he criticizes using the concept-as-oppression model for academic infighting rather than addressing broader social issues.

3
Foundational Values and Real World Challenges

Worldly complications and moral "realism" (*realism* here denotes the opposite of idealism, not a "reality claim") confront the simple and idealistic approach presented above. Basically, two challenges face us. One is how to transfer an interpersonal, small-scale morality to a world of states, labor markets, social classes, and so on—in other words, "scaling up" morality. This effort must acknowledge a range of further difficulties, such as the historical roots of present-day conditions, and also the interface between human arrangements and nature. By small scale I mean social groups that are small numerically, with face-to-face processes; by large scale I mean large numerically, with political and economic hierarchies of such scope that processes often impinge on people anonymously. The other challenge is that how we write processual social science is inconsistent with the demands of constructive writing. Yet processual writing more or less reflects the complexity and historicity of the world. These challenges must be confronted forthrightly; I do not consider them to be insurmountable.

What happens to mutual moral exchange in large-scale societies? People continue to exert and accept interpersonal claims and controls, but only within closed circles of class, kindred, and coalition. Anonymous, often categorical outsiders (i.e., subordinate classes or ethnic groups) no longer have moral claims on the powerful. When such claims fail, large-scale societies develop public immoralities: the application of self-interest unchecked by reciprocal opinions, the inequitable application of state coercion, gross disparities of distribution where some waste resources while others do without, and so on. Such large-scale arrangements are historically developed and, while not unchangeable, do bear the dead hand of the past. (For example, the historical development of ranked ethnic groups, while contingent, is difficult to change.) As social critics responding to large-scale immoralities, we use generalized moral concepts—human rights, basic needs, distributive justice, and so on—all of which are vital but do not spark the direct capacity for empathy that makes us human. How do we offer a framework at a large scale whereby reciprocal morality can overcome or constrain collective immoralities?[1]

This challenge is reflected in the gap between writing in an idealistic vein and writing in processual anthropology. Processual anthropology focuses on the idea that society and culture are constantly mutating relationships, not clear-cut things with names (Wolf 1982). In this perspective, I include political economy, practice theory, and political ecology. We cannot do without the intellectual strengths of processual anthropology. Furthermore, processual anthropology has a politically and morally active origin, the new left anthropology of the 1960s and 1970s (e.g., Hymes 1974; Wolf 1969). Its distinguished proponent, Eric Wolf, offers a humane vision for anthropology (see Wolf 1974:95–97). Yet good processual writing characteristically emphasizes critique rather than constructive morality. First, when it takes apart social and cultural arrangements, its values tend to be implicit rather than explicit—processual anthropology has rarely had a vision of "good power." Second, it tends realistically to identify the causes of problems in the past. Much work focuses on historically deep topics, such as colonialism. Such diagnoses inadvertently displace responsibility from present-day actors.[2] Third, it emphasizes connections, that is, between local suffering and distant markets or powerholders. Connections are important in attributing moral responsibility, especially to actors who remain hidden by distance and wealth. But the web of connections render academic writing overly subtle and vitiate the force of moral vision. Processual social science likewise emphasizes complexity and contingency, which blurs who is responsible for a particular situation and the arena in which change can be taken. The idea of a world system, for example, has this effect, since no single actionable polity corresponds to the dynamics of world capitalism. To speak honestly, radical anthropology has done better at taking apart than putting together again. Yet we cannot do without the analytical power of processual social science as we "scale up" human morality.

As a domain of inquiry, modern international migration offers each of these challenges in abundance (see Kearney 1986, 1991). It is dynamic and large in scale, involving multiple linkages, human, economic, and cultural, across the globe. In its processes, powerful economic interests intersect with the massive bureaucratic nation-state. It stimulates in-group/out-group encounters that often develop into conflicts marked by sharp labor, citizenship, ethnic, and other distinctions. Migrants usually organize themselves as small-scale networks, but they interdigitate with high-level institutions, including globally imbalanced development, transformative capital investments, segmented labor markets, bureaucratized public services, and regional and national politics. Such institutions tend to block the recognition of mutual personhood between hosts and immigrants required for moral interchange. Instead, malignant forms of public debate predominate. Yet migration presents opportunities for alternative social orders. It is a flexible, adaptive process, run on aggregated sets of interpersonal decisions. Networks effectively transmit information and move people. Transnational movement is surprisingly orderly—indeed, a self-ordering process—despite the confusion created by inappropriate and rigid governmental distinctions that render some migrants legal and others illegal. By beginning with migration as a self-regulating and flexible process, we can envision mutual decision-making arenas that bridge the moral barriers between host and immigrant. Thus migration is a bracing test for a processual, complex, power-sensitive constructive anthropology.

The work of Roy Rappaport (1979, 1993, 1995) helps with both dilemmas of this chapter: processuality and moral scale. His work has two basic components: a critique of adaptive disorders, and a vision of a functioning, adaptive system. He suggests that controversies—"troubles," as he calls them—are but symptoms of more profound "disorders," maladaptive relations between basic values and processes (1995:257–281). Lasting change, then, comes from reordering fundamental values. An adaptive system has at its highest levels very abstract, indeed almost empty, sacred postulates (by *sacred* Rappaport means that they go without question). I propose that to reformulate U.S. immigration we need an abstract, democratic bias toward mutual personhood. This contrasts with current, overly specific "sacred postulates" based on culturally and ethnically narrow American nationalism (see Higham 1974; Perea 1997a). I also suggest that mutual personhood override the dominant sacred value of this era, capital accumulation. Sacred values themselves, however, are too vague to regulate immigration. In the proposal I outline below, they are expressed in localistic political encounters between actual people or groups of people, immigrants and hosts, communities and corporations, nested in a sequence of compacts from lower to higher. As the level gets more local, policy decisions become increasingly substantial. This will locate immigration policy in the places and instances where moral reciprocity and conflict (it must be said) are strongest. It will "moralize" it not in the sense of making it "better" but making it *more human*. It also has the effect of making it flexible and locally adaptive (by contrast with the current legalistic policy that struggles to regulate, even halt, those qualities of immigration).

There remains one note of caution. As Rappaport realized, adaptive processes involve human arrangements inside natural systems, rather than closed human systems themselves. The human-species morality discussed before, however, makes no direct reference to the natural environment and does not involve any ideal value of sustainability over time. Immigration debates manifest serious disagreements over human sustainability in the natural environment; thus in Chapter 13 I will counterpose the human ideal vision and the environmental critique. In the long run, we have to use both moralities: as Rappaport writes, "I don't think [that apparent contradictions between humanistic and ecological values are irreconcilable], but their reconciliation is one of the most profound and difficult problems now facing humanity" (1995:255).

Notes

1. The communitarian philosophical position illustrates the importance of thinking clearly about scale and morality. The communitarians, notably Michael Walzer (1983; also see Daly and Cobb 1994:334–336; Whelan 1988), argue for the desirability of nations' closing their borders and restricting immigration. Walzer starts with the idea that morality comes from shared community values, and that the recognition of sharing undermines justifications for internal inequalities. To make a community, however, he argues that it must have some clear grounds for membership. He assumes that nation-state membership is a way of discussing the question of community membership. Walzer characterizes the issues involved in membership by three low-scale, morally reciprocal forms of relationship: "family," "club," and "neighborhood." Each suggests a particular quality of choices about membership in a given moral community: family emphasizes personal sympathy, club the deliberative group choice in admission, and neighborhood the reality that people make communities because they share territories. Immigrants can be justifiably excluded from admission to the club and the neighborhood because of lack of personal sympathy (absence of kinship, cultural similarity, etc.). Walzer does acknowledge that once a nation makes a decision to include and benefit from immigrants, they do have moral standing in the community; he applies this to guestworkers (who he feels should have enduring claims on the host nation). One could infer a similar justification for toleration and inclusion of undocumented aliens who work in and contribute to the U.S. economy. However, I hold a more substantial objection. I agree completely with Walzer's communitarian starting point on morality, for reasons that should be obvious. However, I also hold that such bonds of mutual personhood only work at the low-scale, immediate level. It is a fallacy to attribute the qualities of neighborhoods or families to the level of aggregation of the nation-state. Communitarian language at the level of the imagined "nation" is but a step from drastic nationalism. I hold, instead, that the role of the nation-state is to create and maintain political frameworks that allow local moralities to thrive. The reader should also consult Richard Delgado's critique (1997).

2. The historical perspective also poses the difficult causal and moral challenge of "extrication" (Coady 1991)—how do you reverse an immoral situation in which the key events happened long ago, without acts that violate your values?

4

Recent Immigration to the United States: From Superficial Debates to Underlying Disorders

By cliché, the United States is a nation of immigrants. This is substantially true. What is less well-known is that it is also a nation of anti-immigrants. The two go together, because extensive immigration brings debate over the personhood of new Americans, debates heated by explosive interests and ideologies. This has occurred in the late-18th century, in the 1840s, in the early 20th century, and today. As we proceed through the daunting details of the "new immigration" of the last 32 years, I will offer to the reader a common thread, the revival of anti-immigrationism in conjunction with immigration—the implication being that this is not just an immigration policy recital but an immigration *politics* story as well. Of course, the immigration history itself is important. It involves the evolution of immigration laws and policies, spanning several distinctive types of movement (e.g., refugees and general immigrants). It involves the actual migratory trends, in conjunction with U.S. and global economies. And it involves the various political responses, for example, governmental-study commissions, and a sense of the legal (mostly enforcement) measures that have already been tried with limited results. Out of this entire process, only certain issues emerge as overt controversies. I summarize these obvious policy questions, for they are important and need addressing. But immersed below the waves of policy debates fundamental disorders churn: anti-immigrationism and the breakdown of numerical control. It is through the legal and historical details in this chapter that we recognize these fundamental processes at work. Embarking on this narrative, the reader will need to understand distinctions between legally admitted immigrants, "legal permanent residents," temporary (but legally admitted) visitors and laborers, and illegal or "undocumented" immigrants. The reader also should know that persons given refuge in the United States may be offered temporary protected status or be admitted as legal permanent residents.

The heaviest immigration to the United States, measured as a percentage of U.S. population, occurred from 1890 through 1924. The majority of these immigrants were Europeans, though Mexican and Asian immigration was significant even then. Upper-class Anglo Saxon Americans and others expressed hostility to immigrants through racist ideologies that rejected their shared personhood with Jewish, Italian, and Slavic newcomers, who were viewed as genetically lesser humans (Higham 1974). The immediate consequence of that anti-immigrationism was two laws, passed in 1921 and 1924, that drastically slowed European and Asian entry through biased, often minuscule national quotas for immigrant visas. This closure, together with generational change, assimilation in schools and other institutions, and the mobility brought by economic growth and social redistribution after 1940, encouraged Euro-Americans to forget their immigrant heritage. This hiatus in immigration ended in 1965, with a dramatic legal reform brought about as the final revenge of Jewish, Catholic, and Asian ethnic associations against 1920s immigration discrimination. The 1965 law, because it was nondiscriminatory, offered visas on an equal numerical basis to all nations. It also utilized two nondiscriminatory mechanisms for allocating visas: kin petitions by a small range of specified close consanguineal and affinal kin (the larger set of "preferences") or petitions via occupations, most often by employers (the smaller set of "preferences"). These provisions had the effect of opening the United States to nations where there was a significant demand for visas. Scholars call the people who entered after 1965 the "new immigration." Not only did their numbers rise rapidly, their composition changed from mostly Europeans to Asians, Caribbeans, and Latin Americans (Reimers 1985).

The history of Mexican migration differs, at least until 1965. Mexico has long had an intensive migratory relationship with the United States; this may be one of the most inescapable facts of our entire history. For example, we continue to learn more and more about nonenumerated Mexican immigrant laborers in the pre-20th century industrial west (e.g., Sheridan 1986:35–39, 75–78). When the 1921 and 1924 quota laws were passed, they did not cover western hemispheric migration, because of the political influence of employers of Mexican workers (Bach 1978). Yet Mexican immigrants were also vulnerable to anti-immigrationism. In the Great Depression over a half-million persons of Mexican origin, many of them U.S. citizens, were hounded out of the nation by moralistic local movements (Hoffman 1974). Mexican immigration revived nonetheless after 1940. The postwar era was characterized by a variety of forms of Mexican migration, both permanent and temporary, legal and illegal, together amounting to a significant movement of people. During this period, the United States had a large collectively managed migratory system, the Bracero program of 1942–1965. Braceros were contract laborers without rights to settle permanently in the United States. The Bracero program had notable flaws: its lack of democratic involvement in either nation, its ambivalent place in Mexico, and its "capture" by a small cabal of growers in the United States (Calavita 1992; Galarza 1977). Yet the Bracero system did acknowledge in its own way that the two republics shared a life blood of circulating people. When the United States halted the Bracero program in 1965, the northward movement of Mexican folk did not stop. Their legal standing, however, did change. Some were admitted as legal permanent immigrants, often by petition of their employer, while others came north as undocumented laborers.[1] Despite continuity with the past, illegal entry appeared to be a sharply new phenomenon in how Americans perceived Mexican migration. Although the post-1965 "new" Mexican immigration is different in some ways from earlier periods, current border migration controversies are also an instance of U.S. citizens reacting to their own images and categories about a relatively long-standing and persistent circulation of people.

U.S. refugee policy contributes to the new immigration. During the Cold War era, the United States admitted or refused refugees according to the vagaries of its global interventions (Kahn 1996; Loescher and Scanlan 1986). The earliest refugees were Eastern Europeans, who had little visibility as white Europeans in a low immigration era. When U.S. intervention shifted to the third world, however, refugees were predominantly Latin American, Caribbean, and Asian. These refugees added to the salience of immigration in the public mind. Refugees have fallen into two groups: those who were invited or made welcome on arrival, being favorable to geopolitical aims, and those who sought asylum without invitation, coming as undocumented border crossers, boat people, and so forth. An important surprise, for both government and public, was that the United States could not micromanage these two flows. America had become a nation of "first asylum," the immediate recipient of fleeing masses.

The number of foreign-born persons resident in the United States increased significantly, from less than 10 million in 1965 to more than 22 million in 1993. The proportion of the U.S. population that is foreign born has also risen, though not as dramatically as the aggregate number (Fix and Passel 1994:20–21). Illegal cyclical immigration (where migrants come, work, and leave) also rose during this period, though our grasp of the actual numbers involved is incomplete. More important than the numbers is how they are understood: today, the presence of immigrants is widely felt. On the one hand, a small set of states—California, New York, Texas, Illinois, and Florida—receive masses of immigrants, which makes them highly visible there, yet the new immigration is so sufficiently dynamic and complex that many (perhaps most) communities in the United States have some new Americans. By the 1990s, the whole United States began to resonate with the immigration debates of California. The changing economic and political place of immigrants adds to this basic geography and demography. Before 1965, Mexican cyclical workers were primarily agricultural and western; since 1965, such folk have moved in force into urban and suburban labor markets (Cornelius 1989a, 1989b). In agriculture, such people were harshly bounded by segregation (Menchaca 1995), which made them somewhat unthreatening and invisible. Agribusiness was powerful enough to insist on their presence, despite intermittent opposition. In the new metropolitan situations, Mexican immigrants are more visible, while they lack the shelter of obvious patrons. Groups other than Mexicans have more complicated trajectories, but again they tend to enter rapidly transforming metropolitan contexts, where their presence is politically salient. The sponsored and spontaneous settlement of refugees introduced substantial immigrant groups into areas with few other immigrants (such as Hmong in Minnesota). Finally, besides actual encounters with new immigrants, host Americans receive voluminous media imagery, especially of the Mexican border, giving an exaggerated sense of the size of migration.

The rhythm of immigration anxiety began in the mid-1970s. Initially, most attention was paid to undocumented crossing at the Mexican border. The Select Commission on Immigration Control and Reform (1981) issued recommendations that were, after much struggle, more or less followed in the Immigration Reform and Control Act (IRCA) of 1986. IRCA was the first major effort to alter post-1965 immigration patterns. It sought to continue generous legal immigration but to halt undocumented migration through "employer sanctions." These provisions made hiring an "illegal alien" itself illegal, which had not previously been the case. All employees now have to provide documents to employers to establish that they are U.S. citizens, legal residents, or are otherwise qualified to work. The law, however, encouraged undocumented immigrants to proffer fraudulent documents to employers, thereby letting employers "off the hook," because looking at documents suffices to meet the letter of the law. This negates the effect of the sanctions in stopping illegal immigration. Kitty Calavita (1982, 1990), who long argued that a law interfering with business would prove to be an ineffectual "symbolic law," apparently has been proven correct.[2] The IRCA law also sought to reduce America's covert resident population by legalizing undocumented immigrants with continuous residence in the United States since January 1982. The Special Agricultural Worker provisions, a concession to agribusiness needed to pass the law, legalized undocumented farmworkers under more liberal provisions than the main legalization. The temporary surge in legal immigration (legalization) from IRCA was felt most strongly during the early 1990s; because of this, IRCA probably added to anti-immigrationism rather than resolving immigration debates.

One obscure provision of IRCA did hint at an alternative approach to immigration. The law mandated that a commission look at the global economic causes of unauthorized migration (the Commission for the Study of International Migration and Cooperative Economic Development [1990], or "Ascencio Commission"). Yet their effort to get at root causes was ignored. No politician has mobilized a public movement around the Ascencio recommendations, as they did with the law enforcement recommendations of 1981 and 1994 commission reports. Articulating the relationship of globalization, NAFTA, and immigration was relegated to the nationalist Pat Buchanan. Straightforward connections between U.S. economic policies whipsawing Mexico and upsurges in immigration are not questioned at all.[3] This tells us much about the actual nature of the "debate"—it is not an effort to work with migrants so much as it is an effort to punish (illegal) immigrants.

In the Immigration Act of 1990, the United States reformulated its visa preferences and other clauses governing legal entry. This law, though very important to the technical process of immigration, has had relatively little impact on migratory flows or the political terrain. Since 1994 (in particular, since California's Proposition 187, analyzed later in the monograph), however, the United States has tried forcefully to curtail undocumented immigration. Yet another commission was formed to do yet another study and turn up the volume yet again on immigration anxiety. The U.S. Commission on Immigration Reform (1994) called for a national identity card and "restoring credibility at the border" in its first report. In 1996, Congress authorized doubling the Border Patrol to 10,000 officers in five years. (It had doubled once already over the previous fifteen years.) Congress also authorized turning the existing single-plate steel wall along the San Diego county, California border into a triple wall. Quasi-military INS operations to interdict undocumented immigrants and, indeed, direct military operations on the Mexican border are documented in detail by Timothy Dunn (1996). Another thrust of the 1990s has been taking publicly redistributed resources away from immigrants, no matter what their legal status is. For example, the 1996 welfare and immigration laws cut legal residents off from food stamps and the Supplemental Security Income program (SSI). It merits remarking that most immigrants do not come to the United States for public benefit programs (Fix and Passel 1994:58, 62–63). One feature of current politics is that undocumented border immigrants receive most of the attention, the enforcement, and the anxiety, even though the large majority of "new immigrants" are not Mexican border crossers and are not illegal. It cannot be emphasized too much that U.S. immigration politics persistently confuses the various migrant streams and government responses; people's visceral fear of illegal border migration infects immigration issues as a whole, including legal admissions and refugee policy.

In spite of the political noise and the truly harsh policing, the results in terms of immigration restriction are, at best, ambiguous. In fiscal year 1977 approximately 462,000 legal migrants and refugees entered the United States (U.S. INS 1989:1), while in fiscal year 1996 approximately 900,000 legal migrants and refugees entered (*Migration News* 1997a). Likewise, in 1977 one million arrests were made for unauthorized entry (U.S. INS 1989:109), while in 1996 1.6 million such arrests were made (*Migration News* 1997a).[4] Thus immigration over 20 years has grown steadily, but not in an explosive or invasive manner. Migration has grown *in spite of* the political opinions of Americans, who clearly want to restrict immigration, and in spite of the actual controls embodied in border patrolling and the employment laws. Even the massed enforcement operations of the mid-1990s, pitting thousands of patrol officers against undocumented entrants on the Mexican border, have not succeeded in deterring entry: arrests along the boundary rose from 1993 to 1996, likely from a combination of Mexico's 1994 economic downturn (see note 3), and the Border Patrol paying more attention to undocumented aliens than to drug interdiction, as it had in the recent past. Meanwhile, political efforts to reduce overall legal immigration have stopped in their tracks. For example, Congress split the 1996 immigration act; while the anti-illegal alien provisions (described above) passed easily, proimmigrant employer lobbies emerging in the electronics and computer software industries halted a draft bill reducing the number of legal immigrant visas. As of the time of this writing (1998), the effort to reduce legal entry numbers is unlikely to be revived (*Migration News* 1996, inter alia; Schmitt 1997). Strong anti-immigration opinions (Espenshade and Calhoun 1993; Simon and Alexander 1993) rest side by side with a public policy that welcomes the largest number of legal immigrants in the world. A massive police apparatus, costing a billion dollars a year, has little effect on illegal alien and smuggler networks. There is neither true immigration restriction nor a system that accepts migrant streams for what they are. While immigration in fact has been consistent since the late 1970s (acknowledging some sudden refugee influxes and the gradual evolution of migrant origins), "immigration" in quotes, the public issue, surges forward, powered by anti-immigrationism.[5]

"Immigration" as an issue encompasses four *public* debates. (Any recent reader, e.g., N. Mills 1994, will illustrate these surface controversies.) First, Americans debate the total numbers of immigrants in the

United States, especially the number legally admitted in any given year. We also debate over their characteristics (their national origins, whether they are recruited via kin preferences or employer requests, etc.). Beneath the surface, we argue over the common humanity of immigrants and hosts, expressed in fear of large numbers and objections to Latin American and Asian sources. Second, we debate how to control illegal entry to the United States. This reflects a wider disquiet with the radical dynamism of immigration, and the inability of the nation-state to control it. Third, we debate who should have access to publicly distributed benefits, including medical care, public schooling, and disability or old-age income. Should it be all persons, legal or illegal? Should it reflect the boundaries of the law, including legal resident aliens and citizens? Or should it reflect distrust of foreigners, a special possession only of citizens? In this instance we debate the imagined boundaries of our nation as a community, as Leo Chavez (1992) points out. Chavez (1997) continues this analysis by showing how recent benefit-restriction legislation attempts to reproduce a low-cost, noncitizen Mexican labor force in defiance of their actual transnational residence. Fourth, we debate whether refugees have a special claim on our sympathies, given testimony of their persecution, or whether governmental imperatives prevail over sympathy beyond the border (Gibney 1988). Synthesizing the debates, we find two fundamental issues: frustration with the dynamism and energy of actual migration (which comes across, in a negative way, as anxiety about the failure of simple legal controls), and conflict over the mutual personhood of immigrants and hosts.

Policy debates are vital; it does matter how many people move to the nation in a given year, and what they contribute to our shared life. Anthropologists, as skilled and humane observers, should intervene in these policy-level discussions. Yet to really affect the U.S. political scene, we must understand and change the tone of negativism that pervades the migration debate, the sense of failure and the desire for drastic solutions. Relaxing the moral disorders, even contingently and incompletely, will prove more effective than advocating specific policies when anti-immigrants already have their minds made up. Beyond reacting to it how can we analyze this negative tone?

The negative tone of immigration controversy is a symptom of fundamental disorders. I hold that two disorders, numerical control and anti-immigrationism, are key in their causal importance and their potential for change. The migration laws of the United States rely on "numerical control": numerical targets for finite social types (for example, spouses of U.S. legal residents). Yet such numbers mismatch the social process of migration and inclusion into the host society. Actual migration does not have numerical targets; it relies on innumerable bonds of promise, assistance, and trusting movement among established residents, employers, families, coethnics, and so forth. In real-world migratory situations, people adapt numerical-legal categories to these actual connections when possible, and ignore the law when it does not fit migratory intentions. (For example, the cousins and nephews of legal residents also migrate, although the law makes no provision for them.) Unlike numerical control, actual migration is flexible in who enters and how long they stay, and adapts quickly to the actual niches and labor demands (that is, the realities) of U.S. society. As a result, either the migrant network system manipulates the legal system to its own ends (thus frustrating the top-down social engineering embodied in migration law), or people migrate illegally (thus putting a lie to the numerical limit). The latter distortion in turn causes measurable harms, such as the hundreds of accidental deaths of undocumented immigrants incurred while crossing the Mexican border (Bailey et al. 1996). If current U.S. migration is disordered, the reordering of immigration sought here simulates, but enriches, the naturalistic migration system.

The atmosphere of negativism that pervades the immigration debates, meanwhile, comes from the combination of people's meaningful, if misplaced, anti-immigrationism and the actual dynamism of global migration. I define anti-immigrationism as the hosts' denial of mutual personhood with immigrants, rather than just the opinion that immigrant numbers ought to be reduced. Anti-immigrationism seems purely hostile, but it contains potentially constructive elements. Responding to a democratic deficit in present U.S. politics, it calls for participation in deciding the future development of American communities. But as denial of mutual personhood it narrows participation, while it fails even to obtain its overt goal of slowing migration down. In the process, it reinforces the cost and the power of the U.S. government, operating a police regime with few or no restrictions against moral outsiders, at the Mexican border and elsewhere. The point is not simply to diagnose anti-immigrationism and then assail it, for that would be both undemocratic and deaf to the lessons from criticism of present migration patterns. Anti-immigrationism is as amenable to imaginative social redesign as migration; the burden of mutual personhood and moral regulation can rest as much on host Americans as new Americans. Defending immigrants in a negative climate is unlikely to work; we need to offer the public a vision, a positive alternative that restores the sense of order and moral control. Because anti-immigrationism is the crucial topic in my argument, both critical and reconstructive, I will devote the next chapter to analyzing it at length.

There is a third zone of order and disorder in the interconnectedness of developed (U.S.) and underdeveloped (migrant-sending region) economies and societies: immigration seen as a global system. Saskia Sassen (1988) shows that recent migration to advanced capitalist nations is part and parcel of wider restructurings of production, investment, and labor in the sending *and* host societies. As people's economic and social niches change, they are both displaced and learn of new openings on a global scale. Similarly, migration occurs because stunningly high levels of inequality on a global scale cause ricocheting patterns of environmental degradation and warfare; in this analysis, inequality and expulsive forces do not directly cause labor migration, but such forces do squeeze people through already existing channels (e.g., century-old transportation and labor links between Mexico and the United States [Cardoso 1980; Heyman 1991]).[6] Awareness of the global causes of migration underlies my arguments in the proposal, and I try to remain consistent with this perspective throughout, but I hold that this topic is wider than any one polity can fully affect, even the United States. Thus I cannot usefully present a constructive vision of immigration policy in that frame. Numerical control and anti-immigrationism are points where change in U.S. immigration policy itself can occur. My positions here speak to the humanitarian aspects of migratory movement, the costs to U.S. communities, and the loss of democratic control by those communities. My responses go beyond amelioration, but do not reach as high as the world system. In this I seek a middle ground between the emphatic critique of all existing institutions and the relief of "symptoms."

The proposals contained herein, based on addressing major disorders, revise the terms of the surface debates. For example, local compacts that tax recruiters of migrants to add to the public funding for shared goods (such as public schooling or medical services) address the debate over allocating social distributions to immigrants. Collective allocations thus might calm rather than exacerbate the moral debate over strangers in the society. Similarly, networks can be encouraged to self-regulate and self-limit, an alternative to numerical control with a convincing basis in studies of migration. Social and financial conditions set democratically by communities, not visa targets, might guide migrant self-regulation. The point is not that these are perfect ideas, guaranteed to work, but that they are paths out of our present climate of negativism, a situation that clearly does not work (except, perhaps, for frightening the working immigrants who do manage to come to the United States).

Notes

1. Careful study of Mexican immigrant networks shows that post-1965 legal immigration and undocumented migration originated with former Braceros who maintained relations with U.S. employers (Massey et al. 1987; Mines 1981).

2. The 1996 immigration law made a small gesture at repairing the failed 1986 employer sanctions by authorizing a pilot, voluntary job-applicant identification database for a few immigrant-reliant businesses; unless considerably widened into a national identification card, this is unlikely to have more than marginal effects.

3. For example, over six years leading up to 1994, U.S. fiscal policy-makers encouraged speculative U.S. investors to pour into the Mexican stock market. When Mexico had a relatively small currency crisis in late 1994, the collapse of this outrageous speculative market led to a severe national depression of at least two years length, that in turn led to a significant increase in undocumented immigration. This demonstrates that other capitalist policies, such as those favoring globalization of financial and equity markets, are far stronger than immigration policy in this case.

4. Apprehensions (arrests) of undocumented immigrants rose steadily from 1965 through the late 1970s, fluctuated from 1980 to 1993, and have risen from 1994 onward. About 90 percent of arrested undocumented aliens are Mexican, though the Mexican proportion of the U.S. illegal population is much smaller (see Passel and Fix 1994; Woodrow and Passel 1990). Apprehension statistics are almost meaningless as isolated numbers (for example, 1.4 million arrests in 1995 does not mean 1.4 million illegal aliens tried to cross the border), because an immigration arrest does not necessarily represent an undocumented person. One person may be arrested several times in one year crossing the border, or elsewhere. Other persons may elude arrest altogether. Arrest numbers may roughly indicate trends over time. Even in this there is need for caution; the INS has increased enforcement at the Mexican border, and may well have made more arrests per attempted entry in 1996 than in the past.

5. One can argue that immigration into the United States, as in other advanced capitalist countries, is a labor-supply flow that cannot be controlled or resolved by law because employer interests dominate politics. There is some truth to the labor-supply argument, but it is inadequate as a portrait of politics—why not a finely tuned tolerated labor system then? why all the massive policing aimed at laboring Mexicans? (see Heyman 1998). Since 1965, most laboring immigrants are either illegal and thus are partly obstructed in their efforts to supply their labor, or are admitted through an indirect system of family preferences. This is labor migration, but not labor supply provided in a purely functional manner. While I generally hold that migration politics are more complicated than their labor-supply aspects, there are points where this would be sufficient as an analysis. Although never predominant in the post-1965 era, some employer groups have carved openings in the structure and regulatory application of U.S. immigrant admission law. Agribusiness is well organized for political action and gets results (such as Special Agricultural Workers) in immigration. Similarly, electronics and high-technology sectors represent an emerging lobby in the immigration field (see above). Employer lobbies have enabled the steady admission of groups such as software engineers, nurses, and university faculty. However, most employers of immigrants—gardening firms, restaurants, car washes, janitorial services, light manufacturers—are small, dispersed capital. Their politics is subordinate to more powerful metropolitan capital-coalitions centered on real estate accumulation. In most of these cases, employers and established immigrant employees coordinate information flow, migration assistance, and job prospects within a decentralized process of chain migration. (This will be documented later in the monograph.) They colonize the (noncapital

oriented) legal system rather than overtly dictating to it. Although economic interest is an incomplete analysis of the politics of migration, it is a powerful tool for the analysis of the social process of migration. Since employment in capitalist labor markets is fundamental to network migration, it leads me to my practical approach, which rests on public, democratic control over the powerful and direct mutual commitments of immigrants and employers.

6. The sketch in this chapter of refugees and U.S. foreign policy suggests that another disorder is the international creation of displaced peoples by support of dictators and wars of intervention. Clearly, this can (and I feel should) be changed when it is U.S. responsibility. Nevertheless, U.S. foreign policy ought to be the subject for another monograph.

5
Anti-Immigrationism

U.S. public opinion, polled in mass, strongly favors restricting immigration (Espenshade and Calhoun 1993; Simon and Alexander 1993). Yet mutual recognition of humanity between migrant and host is central to the local-compact proposal. Thus, before we embark on new plans, it is essential to explore the rejection of immigrants, its causes, and its alternate potentials. My model of host-immigrant conflict is not simple; it proposes that political-economic forces have led to national anti-immigrationism, and yet remains aware of tensions in local society and culture. The anthropological perspective is particularly helpful in thinking about immigration conflict at several levels. Anthropology has moved beyond a naive understanding of group membership and cultural contrast; we are aware that political economy and national ideology are important factors in ethnic conflict. Yet our direct fieldwork reminds us that people clash with each other at many levels of aggregation, and that some tension and adjustment may be inherent in immigration.

We can use a simple model of three "scales" in which immigrants and hosts meet. In what follows, the report and individual studies from the Ford Foundation's "Changing Relations" project have been particularly helpful (Bach 1993; Hagan 1994; Horton 1995; Lamphere 1992; Lamphere et al. 1994; Stull et al. 1995). At the face-to-face level, people have their strongest sense of "own-group" membership and distance from other labeled groups. Participants symbolize such tensions by contrasts of lifestyle and daily behavior—language, use of space, and so on. Boundary conflicts delimit direct mutualism among people, perhaps inherently; miscommunication between cultural and linguistic codes, likely in the new settlement situation, exacerbates such conflicts. Both host and migrant individuals provide significant favors, such as leads on jobs and houses, to closely connected others, such as kin, friends, children of friends, long-term coworkers, and so on. Low-scale assistance therefore reinforces immigrant/nonimmigrant fractures (and related ethnic distinctions) when such favors leverage the larger-scale world in the form of unequal job titles and rights, variable consideration by bureaucrats, imbalanced schooling, and so on. In other words, the human moral process, when conducted in a context like the United States, heightens group boundaries.

As we move up in scale, we encounter segmentation: the historical placement of ascriptive groups (i.e., host and migrant "ethnic" groups and genders) in unequal labor markets, capital markets, and political networks (Wolf 1982: 355–363; Lamphere 1992 applies this to the new U.S. immigration). Within the general processes of segmentation, let us highlight "objectification" because of its importance in migration politics. By objectification, I mean the creation of an actionable social "fact" by imaginative reduction of complex actual interactions to a limited label and set of ideas.[1] For example, Kye-Young Park's (1996) essay on Los Angeles shows how immigrant Koreans and host blacks, made tense through everyday give-and-take with each other, worsen their conflict by assimilating the pervasive U.S. racial categories. She also shows how white media portray Korean-black conflict in stereotyped terms. Koreans are portrayed as an entrepreneurial, model minority; this exacerbates tensions with the devalued African American minority. As a social "fact," objectification influences everyday moral reasoning; recognizing and reducing objectification then becomes critical to decreasing the carryover from segmentation to mutual moral regulation.

Objectification occurs within large-scale political economy and ideology, the third level of analysis. Capital is the most radical force in the United States (and, also, the world that sends immigrants).[2] Capital investments bring into communities new persons and businesses, changes the markets for local housing, inserts new actors into the local establishment, or, in other cases, withdraws the employment basis for all these things. Immigrants are often the immediate representatives of the drastic changes that capital brings. When focusing on the impact of radical change, an additional dichotomy is helpful. In specific locales capital injects new migrants, forming the backdrop for the low-scale issues discussed above. Capital also is a disruptive force in the great political arenas of collective membership and felt well-being, such as the state of California and the nation as a whole. It is here that we find the wellspring of bitterness in American anti-immigrationism.

Donald Stull and his collaborators provide a dramatic regional ethnography of capitalist radicalism (Benson 1994; Broadway 1994; Erickson 1994; Stull et al. 1992; Stull et al. 1995). From the late 1970s onward, meatpackers, led by Iowa Beef Packers, reorganized production and marketing, opening gigantic plants in small farm-to-market cities of western Kansas, central Nebraska, the Texas panhandle, and Iowa. Such places could hardly provide the thousands of workers required by the new factories (a labor supply problem aggravated by very high turnover). New immigrants, including Mexican men, some undocumented, and Southeast Asian refugees, soon filled the plants. Workers and their families strained the small meatpacking cities, seeking more housing (met in part by trailer parks), increasing the number of children in schools, straining available medical services, including treatment for extensive occupational injuries, and bringing additional domestic disputes and other duties to small local police forces. Communities changed ethnically, as new Asians and Mexicans penetrated a settled web of Anglo and Mexican Americans. Garden City, Kansas and other towns met the short-run challenges of public schools and services so that, interestingly, low-scale conflict between immigrant and host was muted. But meatpacking firms did not help municipalities cope with change; public "participation" in capitalist restructuring was limited to the counties and states giving concessions (e.g., inexpensive water) to the corporations. Thus the local political process was reactive and dependent. In this context, the immigrants were *apparently* the key problem the community faced. There was no reciprocal interchange of control between community and corporation, and similarly no opportunity for immigrants to come forth in negotiating their own settlement with the host people.

The meatpacking example is too simple to represent all cases of radical change. Heightened Anglo American hostility to new Latino immigrants (especially the undocumented) appears, in some California instances, when new suburban housing invades farming areas (Chavez 1992; Menchaca 1995). Farm owners had dominated local politics, insisting on "tolerance" of the immigrant presence, albeit harshly segregated. Shifts in capital toward real estate development, however, changed the coalitions that dominated local politics; new leaders focused on property values and school district taxation. Intolerant suburbanites then sought to expel the farmworkers, especially attacking their homesites. Meanwhile, the new suburbs attracted other immigrants, providing them jobs as gardeners, domestics, and day laborers, thus heightening the hypocrisy and difficulty of local reconciliation. Whether we look at the Great Plains or the southland of California, transformation causes hostility to immigrants when there is a "deficit of democracy" in recognizing and guiding change; the alternative is an amplified participation that includes immigrants, homeowners, and employers.

What is more important, capitalist radicalism induces reactive xenophobia in the nation as a whole. The United States was the economic and political hegemon of the capitalist world from World War II through the late 1960s. In this era, corporate profits coexisted with nearly full employment (both private and governmental) at increasingly generous pay scales. Expanding governmental redistributions (such as the widening coverage of Social Security) accompanied stable jobs and rising wages. Internationally, the United States aspired to control all major events outside the communist core. A reformist domestic ideal intertwined with a deep sense of global mastery to form a radically triumphalist ideology of U.S. power (Schurmann 1974). This scenario crumbled starting around 1965, as U.S. intervention in world affairs hit limits and capital entered a new period of global competition. Corporate and financial capitalists fought vigorously to reverse the postwar redistribution of wealth. Investors reconfigured their relations with communities, rapidly leaving and entering them; the meatpacking example is archetypical.

In this new context, the perception of disorder has stood out more in U.S. politics than the perception of order. Immigrants are "implicated" in a variety of disruptive changes, both directly and indirectly. The increasing awareness of Americans that the United States engages in diversified global struggles, and not simply a triumphal struggle against the Soviet Union, has made foreign affairs seem less controllable and more threatening. Of course, many new immigrants come precisely from places where the United States has intervened. It is also possible that, in a perceived dangerous and chaotic world, the very idea of foreignness is frightening, and immigrants are condemned by association. The optimism of the postwar liberal era has also eroded domestically. The mass-media delivery of "news," with its tendency to objectify and escalate issues (Best 1995), makes disorders seem massive, multiple, and overwhelming. Let us visualize the U.S. consumer of headline news, receiving the following issues in quick succession: environmental damage, crime, especially narcotics smuggling, terrorism, foreign economic crises, American factory shutdowns, and globalization, racial tensions, and illegal immigration. Among them, immigration stories are reported using the emotionally powerful metaphors of "invasions," "wars," and "floods," relayed through irresistibly dramatic television footage of massed border crossers in the California hills (Chavez 1997; Heyman n.d.[a]). To many Americans, the long list of issues merges into an ambiance of threat and loss.

In this new era, perceived disorder threatens the credibility of the U.S. state and its leadership, its power elites.[3] For example, the 1994 *Report* of the U.S. Commission on Immigration Reform presents as its title, its short-term agenda, and its most urgent recommendation the need to "restore credibility" to U.S. immigration policy, primarily by escalating southern border enforcement. Stuart Hall et al. (1978) suggest that in periods of threatened state hegemony, marginal people are construed as public dangers. Interestingly, this is played out on a thoroughly moralized terrain, in the form of a "moral panic." Moral panics seek to persecute outside "folk devils" (Cohen 1980). Bureaucratic forces of organized policing then attack these "dangers." Mass-mediated public opinion demonstrably reinforces the power of the central state (Ginsberg 1986). In the U.S. case, it reinforces immigration law enforcement.[4]

Substantial evidence supports this analysis. California in the early-to-mid 1990s suffered from a severe recession caused by reductions in U.S. military production, racial conflict in Los Angeles, a distorted taxation system, pollution, earthquakes, fires, and landslides, and the creeping awareness that the state was not destined to grow forever and be the American paradise on earth. The most visible political responses were to attack affirmative action and immigrants. (Zavella [1997] provides anthropological documentation of this process.) Proposition 187, which scapegoated undocumented aliens for California's long-standing budgetary problems, was a classic in the annals of moral panic, combining media-wily promoters with INS connections and prosperous, white grassroots followers (Kadetsky 1994; Stefancic 1997). The panic accelerated when 187 intersected with the television-obsessed election campaigns of Governor Pete Wilson and Senators Diane Feinstein and Barbara Boxer. At the national level, Patrick Buchanan's presidential campaign of 1996 combined blunt criticisms of capital's radical globalism with an urgent desire for repressive discipline at home. Buchanan made masterful use of the symbolism of the Mexican boundary, first stirring up fear of illegal aliens, then offering the reassuring comfort of a border-length wall between "us" and the outsiders (New York Times 1995).

Among the multifarious worries of the day, why does hostility toward immigrants have such an appeal? Given its appeal, is it possible to reverse that sentiment? Certainly, hostility to immigrants is a "cheap" way for politicians to patch up hegemony: outsiders are vulnerable, their employers are not a truly powerful constituency (see note 5, ch. 4), and militarizing the border does not disturb economic interests in a way that, say, restricting capital mobility would. This tells us why the issue is popular with politicians, but less so why anti-immigrationism is a grassroots sentiment. It is instructive in this regard to look at the past. John Higham (1974) and Kitty Calavita (1984) show that America's 1870s–1924 xenophobia occurred during a time of rapid economic growth leading to radical social change, and that the greatest hostility came from established groups (e.g., New England WASP elites) who were threatened by change. As it does today, that era's fervent anti-immigrationism went beyond the hostility found among the direct economic competitors of immigrants. The WASP elite created theories of political and ethnic fear (e.g., eugenics, antiradicalism) that justified their hatred of new Americans. These ideologies were the direct cause of the 1924 cessation of European migration, while the indirect cause was a dynamic economy acting on U.S. society. In the latter 20th century, likewise amidst drastic social and economic change, we encounter related ideologies of incompatible races and cultures (Brimelow 1995; see

Kanstroom 1997; Stolcke 1995), and a newer anti-immigrant ideology, "citizenship." [5]

Citizenship condenses a variety of claims on the state. It includes civil (legal) and political rights, and it may include some strong claims to governmental and corporate redistribution, so-called "social citizenship" (Barbalet 1988; Marshall 1950; Turner 1986). This century's social history shapes the current "citizen" constituencies for immigration restriction. Before 1924, immigrant southern and eastern Europeans were not fully included as citizens. The closing of immigration and the vast expansion of social citizenship from the 1930s onward (especially in the triumphalist post-1945 period), though never fair to blacks, resulted in the "whitening" of Italians, Jews, Lebanese, Greeks, south Slavs, and so forth (Sacks 1994; in general, see Gordon 1964). Assimilation to social and cultural citizenship offers strong positive (though ambivalent) emotions to many ethnic Americans (Newman 1993:68–71). As a result of these processes, both older and newer "whites" feel different from new immigrants.

Paul Blumberg (1980) characterized the present epoch as "inequality in an age of decline." Many white citizens "own" an eroding claim on the U.S. polity and economy (see Katherine Newman's [1993] ethnography of suburban New Jersey). Their position is *possessive citizenship*, my usage following C.B. Macpherson's (1962) history of "possessive individualism" in market democracies.[6] Citizenship, even possessive citizenship, has active moral qualities, a sense of worth and constructive involvement, a sense of redistribution and decent quality of life. The mid-20th century elaboration of upward mobility and American triumph had a high moral tone, for example. But citizenship as a moral concept implies that noncitizens are moral outsiders, through forms of symbolic reasoning well-known to anthropologists (see especially Douglas 1966 on the boundaries between purity and danger). If citizenship includes a positive moral claim to redistributive benefits, for example, then citizens might see, in a period of decline, undocumented immigrants receiving emergency medical care or public education as dangerously immoral. This is exactly the content of Proposition 187, and the related federal welfare law of 1996 that eliminated food stamps, Social Security disability, and old-age pensions for legal immigrants.

Empirical evidence about anti-immigrants supports these arguments strongly. Wayne Cornelius (1982) studied a collection of letters and their writers who expressed opposition to Mexican immigration. The writers were neither direct competitors with nor large-scale employers of aliens. Instead, anti-immigrationists were (modally) older persons, whites, males, white collar or skilled blue collar workers, living in California but originally from the Midwest or South, and holding an isolationist worldview. They worried about a generalized loss of law and control, including loss of control over borders and other nations. For them, national loyalty combined with the idea that the system is not working anymore.

California public opinion polls support Cornelius's findings. Strong elements of opposition to immigration are "symbolic" rather than direct material conflicts (Espenshade and Calhoun 1993; on symbolic politics in immigration, see Calavita 1982, 1984). Poll items that indicate symbols of American nationalism include emphasis on the English language, fear of declining social services and benefits, a sense of worsening crime, and pride in America as a land of opportunity (Espenshade and Calhoun 1993:203–206, 209–210). Legality is an important symbol. Persons with anti-immigrant views assume that most recent U.S. immigrants are illegal (Espenshade and Calhoun 1993:192; this is not, in fact, true—see Fix and Passel 1994:21–23). David Hayes-Bautista, Werner O. Schink, and Jorge Chapa's (1992) study of the generational conflict between the young families of new immigrants and the aging white population also supports the historical model of anti-immigrationism, since it places anti-immigrants in the following time sequence: raised after the 1924 immigration cessation, shaped during the post–World War II social compact, and disturbed by its post-1965 breakdown and new immigration.

The people described by Cornelius have few ways to voice their opinions about the destruction of the social compact in America. The United States has lost much of its strong party system and has a weak public sphere; the current concept of democratic participation is voting in mass (Kushma 1988; MacLennan 1994; Turner 1990). Margaret Shannon (1990) suggests that rumor, bluff, and the media are characteristic *informal outlets for participation* in the absence of formal means of participation and when the relation to the target of participation is impersonal. Chavez (1992) provides fascinating ethnography of such participation in public meetings in north San Diego county. A group of new suburban "possessive citizens" sought to harass and expel small informal settlements of Mexican and Central American undocumented immigrants. They succeeded in shattering the community of Green Valley. Rumor, such as fear of diseases and the harassment of schoolchildren, was pervasive. Local politicians, reporters, and public meetings helped broadcast the symbols of objectification and exclusion (as Chavez points out, even spoken by sympathetic outsiders). Meetings offered no opportunity for participation of immigrants, though they did provoke protests by proimmigrant activists. An interesting character, Fred Bright, a local farm manager, allowed the undocumented immigrant community to reside on his lands and had a mutual moral relation with the community.

But Bright's potential for mediating exchanges between hosts and immigrants was unrealized in this distorted version of participation.

Chavez documents an important moment in U.S. history, for suburban San Diego county is a wellspring of California and U.S.-wide anti-immigration movements, and of the militarization of the Mexican border. The local moral negotiation was difficult enough, but San Diego–based political entrepreneurs (e.g., Pete Wilson, who began as Mayor of San Diego) amplified the issue to the national arena. The single most important direct result of California's 1994 moral panic was the initiation, at the federal level (by President Bill Clinton and Attorney General Janet Reno), of a massive Border Patrol operation on the western San Diego county–Tijuana border. It reverberated in 1996 in the form of legislation authorizing the doubling of the Border Patrol to 10,000 officers, and the introduction, as a serious political suggestion, that the military take over border immigration enforcement. This escalation of local or regional issues into a simpleminded, large-scale solution—massive immigration control—is a perfect example of Rappaport's disorder of "hypercoherence" (1979:162). Hypercoherence is the elevation of low-level questions into systemic obsessions (e.g., border control) in ways that drastically overstate their importance as "issues." Unfortunately, escalation of immigrant-host conflict definitely characterizes U.S. migration politics.

The political level at which solutions must be sought exacerbates negativism. Immigration, by existing law, is almost purely a federal issue; the means that we now rely on to change migration are also mostly national. (Some are statewide, as in California, but that vast state has extracommunity, "mass" politics, similar to the national level.) Americans do participate in collective immigration decisions, though not in equal and fair ways, but they do so in ways that elevate conflicts into abstract hatreds: thus the tendency toward national-level solutions. To localize immigration conflict and resolution is a risky step, very risky indeed (see chapter 8), but it is needed to avoid the almost military level to which immigration conflict now reaches.

Given the strength of anti-immigrationism, given the complexity and depth of its causes, can the ethical terms of immigrant-host relations change? Can moral panics be made moral exchanges? The pattern of insider mutuality and routine separation between hosts and immigrants will be difficult, perhaps impossible to change. Much local friction and bias will be inevitable. The idea of the local-compact system is not that immigrant-host conflict will disappear but that escalation and hypercoherence will be avoided. The local-compact approach will seek two ends: to obligate the host community to do various acts with respect to immigrants, thus setting up a regular moral interchange between otherwise segmented immigrants and hosts, and to require that decisions be made locally, thus reducing the escalation of conflict.

In regard to whether immigration reform can really change cultural and social conflict, we learn much from the recommendations of the "Changing Relations" project board (Bach 1993). The first lesson is that just a bit of moral interaction may suffice for many situations—just enough to convince the various immigrants and hosts of their basic ground rules for mutual tolerance. Given this initial moral assumption, mutual "indifference" would probably help, as F. G. Bailey (1996) has shown for avoiding ethnic violence in India. His study suggests the danger of intense moral crusades, resembling the ones I have described for U.S. nationalism, and the virtues of low-key moral and pragmatic interchange. The Changing Relations Board found precisely that segmentation, in which immigrant and host groups lead fairly separate lives, avoids much conflict.[7] The second lesson from the Changing Relations Board is that when hosts and/or varied immigrants focus on a mutual concern that leads them to a common institutional nexus, such as tenant organizations facing shared problems with landlords, they do reach "accommodation." The local-compact systems would widen such opportunities since hosts and immigrant-ethnic associations would share the regulation of petitioning and settlement.[8]

Interesting evidence suggests that I am not overly indulging in wishful thinking when I suggest that face-to-face contact in the local compacts would increase recognition of mutual personhood and decrease objectification between hosts and immigrants. The U.S. public chooses immigration restriction when polls ask abstract and general questions about policy (Espenshade and Calhoun 1993; Harwood 1986b; Simon and Alexander 1993). Edwin Harwood, however, found that "Americans respond very differently to illegal *immigration*, which is an issue in which the immigrant is faceless and unknown, from the way that they do to illegal *immigrants*" (1986a:209, emphasis in the original). Espenshade and Calhoun cite an interesting 1984 study that found that "despite exhibiting generally negative feelings toward immigration, majorities of [respondents] supported admitting each of 10 imaginary individuals whose profiles match those of typical entrants to the United States" (1993:198). The profiles approximate the actual learning about other people that should take place in a context of reciprocal moral exchange. The moral exchange envisioned in the alternative policy would go beyond host-immigrant contacts; it would include local and regional constraint on and moral interchange with employers, investors, metropolitan elites, and so on to tame capitalist radicalism.[9]

If my analysis is correct, anti-immigrant politics, with its extremely objectified moral solutions, is a symptom of disorderly capital and U.S.

global politics. Critical social scientists have made much of the social construction of inequalities and ideologies in recent years, but what is deconstructed can be reconstructed differently.[10] The repair of our misplaced moral responses would begin with obligatory negotiations with investors and developers over openings for and costs of new immigrants. For example, local compacts that tax employers to widen the total pool of redistributable resources would revise the political struggle in California over education, health, and other social benefits to immigrants, illegal and legal. The proposed approach would act not just on the level of taxes and costs, but also on the ideological level of restoring the citizenship ideal in the face of capitalist radicalism. It would open a new path to citizenship, a sense of participation in and control over events, making hosts and immigrants cocitizens when they negotiate together over claims on capital and the state.

Notes

1. I take *objectification* from Daniel Miller's (1994) work on Trinidad, where the condensed ethnic categories East Indian and black possess lives of their own, channeling who is and is not included in low-scale mutual moral regulation and altruism (also see Yelvington 1993, 1995).

2. On capitalism as a radical force, see Scott 1985, Wolf 1969.

3. The modifier *perceived* is important: the world may inherently be disorderly (Rosenau 1990; Rosenau and Durfee 1995), but its perception as such threatens politicians' tactics and the public's sense of a decent life.

4. Let us note, in analyzing how immigration becomes an objectified issue within this sense of anxious disorderliness, the importance of the symbol of lawfulness and the impact of the idea of "illegal immigration." As many people have noticed, there is a highly visible gap between law and reality in immigration (Cornelius et al. 1994). (Given the flaws of numerical control, the existence of this gap is not surprising.) Why is this gap so disturbing, if it serves the interests of employers and consumers of migrant labor? Ethnographers find a complex set of American ideas about lawfulness, among them the notion that law involves definitive rules and processes. Law has great legitimacy but it is high in scale, and applied to distant others (Greenhouse 1989). This perception exacerbates public dissatisfaction with U.S. immigration policy and tells us something of the unsatisfactory scale where we now look for solutions. The faithful in law confront the media-constructed "reality" of immigration, that out-of-control illegal border crossers and waves of new arrivals are making a "mockery" of "our" immigration system. (When advocates of immigration law enforcement focus on the gap between law and "reality" in immigration [a reality often phrased as "out-of-control"], we should not forget that the publicized "reality" differs from the "really real" social processes of migration, a consistent theme in ethnographies [e.g., Chavez 1992] and statistical treatments [e.g., Fix and Passel 1994].)

5. In my analysis, then, conflict between immigrants and hosts is not exclusively about political economics. But capitalist radicalism in the broader

view explains the patterning of conflict: the rapid change in local social relations, the growth of new immigrant communities, the defensive role of citizenship ideology, and so on.

6. This discussion of possessive citizenship is paralleled by Linda Bosniak's (1997) very interesting analysis of the term *nativism* as delimiting insiders and outsiders in immigration debates.

7. The Changing Relations Board (Bach 1993) reports that the absence of any accumulated recognition—as in the present U.S. immigration system—meant that when immigrants and hosts did intersect (for instance, in schools or in job title disputes), then they conflicted. Media coverage of "ethnic battlelines" worsened the situation because it objectified conflict. Clearly, each of these negatives have converse positive messages about how we can do things differently, as outlined in the text.

8. Segmentation in labor markets, organizations, and so on plays an important role in immigrant-host conflict, and in further ethnic rivalries. It is important to move engaged anthropology from an awareness of segmentation to positive visions of how to alter or tame it. For my purposes, I treat it as a more-or-less inherent part of large-scale economic production and bureaucratic control. The plan works within segmentation, since (for example) it actively supports recruitment of immigrants via networks into employment and residential niches.

9. In anthropology, the legacy of Karl Polanyi (1957) has been fairly apolitical, and only implicitly critical. In the approach here, I draw on the political side of Karl Polanyi's critique of socially uncontrolled capitalism.

10. If we accept a tight power- and social-construction analysis, then we cannot balk at the demand that we crack it apart and rebuild it. Our response might well be radical (in the sense of being quite different from the status quo), but it would be intentionally constructive. In saying this, I draw on an interesting radical, constructive literature on crime from Britain that followed Stuart Hall et al.'s outstanding deconstructive work (Hall et al. 1978; Kinsey et al. 1986; Matthews and Young 1986; Taylor 1981; but see criticisms in Cohen 1985; Gilroy and Sim 1987).

6

The Basic Plan: Recruitment and the Receiving Situation

Two ideas are at the heart of my proposal: that immigration numbers, sources, and so on (what I shall call recruitment) should be open-ended and flexible, and that local reception of immigrants should regulate this open-ended process. The latter would involve internalizing social costs into recruitment. The former idea (recruiting) is the main subject of this chapter, and the latter (the local compacts) the subject of the next one. To fully comprehend the plan, ideas from both chapters ought to be combined, but of course, I cannot present everything at once, so I beg the patience of the reader as I leave participation, moral toleration, and collective expenditures for later. Here, I mainly address what will replace the current system of migration control in a new arrangement of petitions, visas, residential rights, and citizenship. The approach is not only to reshape the decisions of immigrants but also the decisions of the receiving society. Before we can discuss this approach, however, we need to review the existing regulations that make up "numerical control."

Numerical control sets quantitative targets (ceilings, usually) in kin, employment, and asylum categories and provides immigrant visas within those target categories on a first-come, first-serve basis. The ceilings are inflexible, the categories cannot be extended or modified (e.g., to petition for cousins rather than sons or daughters), and, most important, numerical approaches pay no attention to the local community's degree of commitment to having that individual, with specific job or kin ties, immigrate. Since numerical control does not adjust to demand, immigration "preferences" (quotas) from particular nations become oversubscribed and build up lengthy queues. Most important, numerical control is an "illusion," to use the telling term offered by John Scanlan (1982).

If numerical control worked, it would clearly determine which immigrants come; it would accurately represent the will of the democratic polity, as applied to numbers and types of new residents. As Scanlan characterizes it, however, current numerical control is but the "front door" of actual migration. Those migrants who cannot enter through the front door instead enter through the "back door" of undocumented migration. Therefore, numerical control does not effectively enact the public will, which in turn heightens public frustration with migration as a whole. To get some idea of the numbers involved, legal immigration (other than one-time legalization) was approximately 800,000 annually in the early 1990s (Fix and Passel 1994:22). Fix and Passel (1994:4) estimate that the net annual growth of the U.S. undocumented population is 200,000–300,000 for the early 1990s. This does not include the much larger temporary (cyclical) flows of undocumented entrants. There is a third, "executive door" as Scanlan terms it: refugee admissions. A ceiling set annually, in advance, by Congress and the Presidency partly determines the width of this door. Also, persons who first come to the United States (as undocumented immigrants or temporary visitors) and then obtain asylum go through this door (in a sense, the "back door" of refugee policy). Refugees and asylees amounted to roughly 100,000–150,000 per year in the early 1990s (Fix and Passel 1994:22). The point is that numerical control, which counts only the official "front doors," simply does not delineate actual migratory numbers.

Instead, the immigrants themselves, their employers, and their kin—not the formal intentions of Congress—determine the volume of actual U.S. immigration. Formal legal migration is but one option, though the preferred one, for migrants who chose to come to the United States. We know this because when legal entry is unavailable, migrant decisions are demonstrably unaffected. For example, the "front door" of legal immigrant visas should determine who settles *permanently* in the United States, if it has any meaningful role at all. Yet there is in the United States a significant group of undocumented "settlers," people who reside permanently or over a long period without legal admission as such (see Chavez 1988; Chavez 1992; Chavez et al. 1990).

Numerical control *cannot* work, and the social science of migration tells us why. Michael Piore (1979) provides a fundamental model of labor migration, the largest type of movement.[1] Piore suggests that immigration is not just a natural result of the supply of poor people and the demand for them by wealthy nations. Migration is actively started by employers who recruit outside their society in order to find economically naive and politically weak laborers. Formal, numerical migration is sometimes important during this initiatory stage (e.g., U.S. toleration of Western Hemispheric migration in the 1920s and the Bracero Program in the 1940s–1960s). The migrants themselves soon take an active place in Piore's model, however. They start by targeting short periods of temporary work in the host society. Their goals are those of a simple-minded "economic man" in the host society, sojourning to make money, but their motives in the home nation are rather more subtle and social. (Piore suggests that they use migrant income to alter their subordinate position in local social hierarchies.) Because immigrants have such motivations, they soon take the initiative in migration (e.g., perpetuating Mexican migration after 1965 via undocumented border crossing). Governmental numerical control becomes increasingly irrelevant. Furthermore, people settle out of migrant streams. The generation raised in the host location assimilates the new social valuations of jobs, money, and so on, and thus leaves behind their immigrant frames of reference. They become "permanent residents" whether or not the host nation has a numerical, legal structure for admitting them as permanent residents.

In "applying" the Piore model, capitalists and immigrants make hash of unchanging numerical controls. The best that can be said is that they sometimes use the legal forms while ignoring the intent of the laws. If the legal form does not serve their purpose, they bypass legality altogether. Massey et al.'s (1987) study, alluded to earlier, provides striking proof: U.S. employers initiated Mexican labor migration through the Bracero program until 1965 and sponsorship of legal immigrants after that date. Sponsored west Mexican villagers chose the later migrants who came to the United States: their brothers and sons, poorer cousins, and fellow villagers. Some of them "colonized" the legal categories, while others, who did not fit the kinship preferences, came anyway by illegally crossing the border. Migrants of all categories (but especially the more secure, legal ones) settled in the United States, adopting U.S. labor market roles and expectations. In the process, they renewed the demand for new temporary migrants, now mostly undocumented. Faced with such protean developments, no simple system of control is likely to succeed (Portes 1983); inflexible regulation from above becomes a source of disorder, not order, in adaptive systems (Rappaport 1979, 1993, 1995).

If not top-down numerical control, then what? The alternative immigration system would start with local (immigrant and host decisions) in order to be flexible. Migration policy's main role would be to set up the conditions for those decisions, not their end points. Then, aggregation of diverse local outcomes would result in a national migration "policy." There would be no national ceilings, preferences, or quotas. Local compacts would set immediate numerical targets and qualitative terms of entry, in direct consultation with publics, employers, and migrants. Compacts also would set the rules for legal recruitment by employers, coethnics, or other sponsors, including the payment of local social costs. Recruiters could petition for persons of any kinship or personal relationship, or employment quality, within the policies and restrictions of their particular local compact. In other words, there would be no specific categories of admission, no national origins restrictions, and so forth. The nation as a whole might retain some general exclusions, though—for example, not allowing the admission of persons with violent or aggravated felonies. The INS would process the visa petition, and the approved visa would provide for permanent residence. In other words, a petition would commit to paying for permanent settlers, a requirement that will undoubtedly rest heavily on the decisions of local compacts. All immigrants would be permanent residents with full legal rights and privileges in the United States. People might move back and forth from the home nation, but there would be no temporary, contract, or any other less-than-complete membership in the United States. (Permanent settlement and the place of transnational migrant peoples will be discussed in chapter 9.)

Because certain features of the new plan dramatically differ from the status quo, it is worth reviewing the contrasts in some detail. The scheme would eliminate the kin preference system of ranking admissible immigrants. Legal migration would follow the greater complexity of real networks. Acceptable relations might include more distant kin, hometown mates, and even friends. These connections would require distinct petitions to the local compacts. Visas, however, would include the "family reunification" of spouses, minor children, and parents over the age of 65 for the petitioned immigrant; this would affect the cost structure (e.g., anticipating settlement of these people) of the local compact. These provisions would overcome the characteristic failing of the current kinship preferences that migrants come to the United States illegally when the law does not match their network relationship. The new plan would also eliminate the current occupational preferences—or, better said, it would extend them to the entire migration system.[2] The occupational preferences have not worked very well—in fact, most occupational visas go to family members of occupationally petitioned entrants, and many occupational visas are left unused (Migration News 1995, 1996)—while the reality is that employment attracts most kin and undocumented immigrants, except refugees. The local-compact system assumes that there is an integral fusion of employment with kinship recruitment networks, and that one petition can acknowledge both elements.

The new plan also would abandon the national origins system, in which every nation in the world can receive up to 7 percent of preference visas (25,620 visas subject to the global admissions ceiling [Interpreter Releases 1990:1357]). The proposal to eliminate uniform national quotas should be set forth with trepidation. The present law, enacted in 1990, is based on the 1965 principle of equitable treatment by national origin for all migrants. The 1965 act was a momentous rejection of prejudice in American nationhood, overturning the racist 1921 and 1924 Immigration Acts that forbade Asian immigration and embodied eugenic interpretations of superiority of northern Europeans over southern and eastern ones. Thus I emphasize that the new proposal would not bring back unfair origins restrictions. It does not limit the immigration of any nationality at all. It does abandon, however, the idea of numerical control by national origin. The 30 years since 1965 show that the equal national quotas do not adequately match the demand for migration via specific recruitment paths that are very unequal among nations. Some nations, such as Mexico, the Philippines, India, and the Dominican Republic, have visa delays lasting years (Stapleton 1991:377). We could abandon the equitable but awkward national origins system without retreating to a consciously discriminatory quota system by recognizing that sources self-regulate because of recruitment of fellow nationals, gradually modulated by the addition or attrition of source countries when key individuals enter or quit the recruitment process.

Since there would be no total ceiling for annual admissions, numbers of new Americans would vary by the aggregated petition demands of particular immigrant families, employers, and other organizations (such as coethnics). Does this plan call for open immigration with unlimited numbers? Would the United States be flooded? The answer is no. The plan could control numbers of legal admissions through the imposition of substantial costs of settlement in a locally participatory plan. It differs from the status quo not in the size of demand to migrate to the United States, but in the crucial idea that responses among immigrants would regulate migration more effectively than a clumsy numerical limit incompletely enforced by bureaucrats. For example, if typical immigrant recruiters such as restaurants paid substantial social taxes, they would try to stay within the locally set numerical limits. The recruiter would also spread the discouraging word through existing migrants to potential ones (hereby utilizing the power of network migration), lest they also become the recruiter's responsibility. The strengths and weaknesses of feedback for regulating the scale of migration into the United States are discussed in chapter 12, where I consider ethnographic observations on actual information transfer and consequent migratory decision making.

I do not advocate the flexible-recruitment/local-compact system on abstract principles or impassioned rhetoric, however; the proposal's power, and its flaws, are illuminated best against the backdrop of actual ethnographic cases. In particular, I ask how the putative arrangement would encompass the great variety of observed migrant recruitment and mobility. We are fortunate to have David Griffith and Ed Kissam's (1995) *Working Poor*, a multisite study of farmworkers whose theme is the diversity of local scenarios. For perishable crops in Maryland and Delaware (Delmarva), and North Carolina, individual farmers recruit steady annual migrants, often couples; sometimes they support more permanent settlement of valued workers with housing and personal assistance. Short-term, peak-labor needs are filled by male workers, often lateral kin (e.g., cousins) of core-worker families. Sometimes farm-labor contractors supply short-term workers. Delmarva draws on a laborers who winter over in Immokalee, Florida. This group is currently mostly Mexican, but it includes other domestic and immigrant laborers. Florida's agriculture has fragmented recruitment patterns because it is a cheap residential haven and job center utilized by many different groups. Its labor market is marked by the on-the-spot formation of labor crews. Kinship and network are still important, but labor contractors are particularly strong in this context. Michigan summer harvesting resembles Delmarva in its personalized employer-worker relations and paternalistic approach to housing; it is linked to winter residential settlements in the lower Rio Grande Valley of Texas. There, long-term, gradual immigration from Mexico to the United States takes place with little governmental or other social support for the costs of settlement in the new nation (e.g., with little infrastructural support for self-constructed housing). Finally, Parlier, California resembles the Florida situation in being a center for constant migrant influx and turnover. It is less plagued (apparently) by labor bosses; instead, it emphasizes the recruitment role of immigrants themselves. These involve both strong kin networks with key central actors and a "chaotic and weaker set of network relations," in which male migrant workers with similar needs for jobs and shelter opportunistically form "switchboard households" (Griffith and Kissam 1995:217).

Let us now take Griffith and Kissam's findings, and lay out schematically how the new proposal would handle different types of migration. The migration plan would be simplest when an employer petitions for a permanent or regular cyclical employee who is already known through networks, undocumented migration, or temporary residence; it would bring that process into the open, and through the compacts formalize the elements of paternalism that already occur in Michigan, Delmarva, and North Carolina (e.g., Griffith and Kissam 1995:70–71). When employers seek to widen their recruitment range beyond core workers, the employer and the existing immigrant worker could jointly petition for kin or other acquaintances, with the specific connection left indeterminate as long as the overall terms of the compact are followed. This follows everyday practice in which existing employees broker new hires, and provides for extension of the permanent workforce and supply of temporary "peak" workforces. An employer, however, may not want to support the entire cost of permanent settlement for a temporary laborer; thus every compact would have to have an arrangement by which such workers enter a labor pool sustained by multiple employer contributions to the compact as a whole. There would also have to be labor interchange arrangements between compacts, such as between Florida and Delmarva, or Texas and Michigan. Interchange is a dauntingly complex element of the compact system, I must admit; but multilocality is a reality of immigration and arranging transferable or rotating responsibility for the social costs of immigrants (e.g., settlement housing and services) would be needed over the long run.

A second typical path of migration is relatives arriving to stay with immigrated kin "on speculation" of finding work and possible settlement. The proposal would initially place the compact costs of these migrants on the host family, much like the current U.S. immigration system that requires all kin petitioners to assure income support for petitionees for five years. Unlike the current system, however, which is a promise rather than an actual paying into the system, there would be real payments to the locality. Costs would switch from the host family to the employer when employment for the new arrival is secured. Furthermore, many "speculative" kin immigrants come without documents (for example, see Mahler 1995). In the new system, some might continue to enter without documents to avoid costs, but the flexible scheme would encourage and facilitate legalization of these persons as they secure work. By contrast, in the current scenario, a family petition may take years. It becomes a legal formality, less important than the fact that speculative migrants arrive, obtain work, and settle down with or without papers.

A third path is mass unconnected migrants, such as the men in Parlier looking for temporary work who form switchboard households. Many of these people have kin, hometown, or past employer connections, and thus a mechanism outlined above would encompass their case. Their connections, however, may not be to a stable employer but to a formal or informal labor broker (e.g., a farm labor contractor). To function effectively, the local-compact system must make claims against labor brokers and contractors, not an easy task. Given their slippery track record, the following system makes the most sense. The entire process of worker arrival at brokerage locations might be unregulated since it seems difficult to control in detail. But if an employer directly or indirectly, through a contract, hired a worker, that employer would have to start the petition and payment process for the individual worker. The petition and payment would cover a general "brokered worker" status. Every time the worker switched jobs, the requirement to pay compact taxes would go to the new employer. (The definition of employer would be the farmowner above the labor contractor.) Such payment arrangements could be tracked and then billed after the fact of employment, since the ethnography (Griffith and Kissam 1995:48–49) shows that personal job information and labor brokers work far more efficiently than official job referral banks. Receipts would go to both local compacts and intercompact regional arrangements. A key expenditure in the regional system would be to fund social services in migrant assembly communities, such as Indiantown and Parlier. Such places bear particular burdens of absorbing large temporary influxes of migrants, and/or housing workers and families during off-seasons. Our present society handles these seasonal, uneven burdens hardly at all, leading to very poor conditions of life. A new arrangement can ameliorate that.

The flexible migration plan builds on the experience of transnational migration between Mexico and the United States. Because movement between the two countries is straightforward, it has allowed complex settlement and cycling patterns, even under the current arrangements that divide immigrants between legal and illegal categories. Wayne Cornelius (1987–90) and Luin Goldring (1987–90, 1996) report on three migrant-sending communities in western Mexico. Las Animas, Zacatecas and Tlacuitapa, Jalisco present the expected pattern, in which most men work in the United States temporarily and reside permanently in Mexico. When men and women do settle and incorporate into the United States, they abandon residence in Mexico except occasional visits and possibly for retirement. In Gomez Farías, Michoacan, however, a large portion of the community sustains cyclical residence in both nations, living and working in Watsonville, California during the agricultural season there, and living in Gomez Farías in the off-season. The Gomeño pattern may happen because the state of California provides inexpensive but seasonal migrant housing in Watsonville; it may also be attributable to the particulars of landholding and investment in Gomeño strawberry agriculture. It results in the population with the lowest education of the three Mexican towns, and the fewest investments in businesses in the hometown. The Gomeño experience may offer some insight into the effects of subsidized housing and open access in the alternative migration plan that might underwrite such sustained binational adaptations. We cannot be certain if Gomez Farías is predictive, however, because of the several unusual factors in that case. The three-village study shows, at any rate, that border entry and citizenship rights must be flexible, for it would be better to encompass than to battle such a range of variation.

The proposal here would handle transnational movement more adequately than the present system of numerical control involving narrowly defined status. The current legal position of "permanent resident" does not forbid cyclical international movement, but also does not adapt to it. The new arrangement's visas would be permanent, even for immigrants initially planning only temporary residence. This would anticipate the fact that some cyclical immigrants eventually would settle in the host society; it would ensure that such settlement be legal and secure. The costs of such an immigrant visa would, of course, have to reflect longer-term planning by the compact than employers or immigrants themselves are likely to make. A permanent immigrant visa also would facilitate transnational movement since it would make regular movement between the United States and the source nation open and secure. Finally, a permanent visa would open the legal path of naturalization to U.S. citizenship.

Let us examine the components of citizenship, as outlined earlier. The permanent immigrant visa would, in itself, convey full civil rights—that of the legal resident—as it does in present U.S. law (while grounds for deporting legal residents may deserve some reform, the basic notion of civil rights for legal residents is already in place). The local-compact system would distribute varied economic and social goods among citizens and petitioned immigrants, thus including immigrants with hosts within a more encompassing (if locally determined) concept of social citizenship. The question of political citizenship, the right to participate and vote, is more complicated. I suggest a two-fold path consistent with the idea of local compacts: immediate rights to local political participation, with state and national participation being longer-term and contingent on actively choosing to naturalize. This change requires less altering the letter of U.S. naturalization law than the spirit in which citizenship is given.

Legal resident (immigrant) members of the local compact should have representatives in ongoing negotiations and administrative oversight. On the other hand, naturalization should convey political rights to participate in elections for extralocal offices. A longer period of residence (say, five years) would be required before a legal resident naturalizes to U.S. citizenship. Willfully chosen naturalization is a sign of incorporation into U.S. society (see chapter 9). The new immigration plan would maintain current U.S. law that gives citizenship to any children born in the United States, since having children in the host nation is a key step during incorporation (Chavez 1992:175–177). (A more complex system would start with the presumption of birth citizenship, but reduce its availability to children who grow up outside the United States.)

Historically, the bureaucratic process of naturalization has been slow because the INS and the politicians who set its priorities were preoccupied with the small risk that potential citizens were subversive or had a nefarious criminal or immigration violation record (fundamentally, reflecting the "possessive" concept of citizenship). Naturalization conducted as a quasi-criminal investigation causes tremendous delays. Both the United States and Mexico have recently removed barriers to naturalization: the United States by reducing some bureaucratic obstructions to obtaining naturalization, and Mexico by legalizing dual citizenship. (Many Mexican immigrants had not been willing, in the past, to give up their Mexican citizenship to obtain the U.S. one.) Immigration restrictionists, however, have viewed the recent U.S. simplification of naturalization with considerable hostility, the proximal issue being that a few immigrants with criminal records are naturalized. These naturalization reforms should be continued and the hostile reaction to nationalization resisted. We should accept dual citizenship and favor U.S. naturalization because it reciprocates the immigrants' growing commitment to the United States. In the new arrangement, there would be little reason to become a citizen just to get social benefits, since such distributions would be available to noncitizens registered to a local compact as well. Citizenship would then be a real sign of commitment. In a world of transnational migrants, with a flexible recruitment system that allowed long periods of cyclical migration with low commitment, naturalization would be a positive statement of moral incorporation, not a precious possession to be fearfully guarded.

The flexible immigration plan fits the increasing importance of transnational political relations, including cross-border relations between governmental entities below the nation-state. The local compacts, in regulating specific recruitment networks and dealing with transnational peoples, would deal with national and local governmental officials and nongovernmental associations in sending nations. This is both a problem and a promise. As a problem, it would require sophistication for which U.S. municipalities are scarcely prepared. As a promise, it would offer more effective means for immigrant communities to regulate the behavior of U.S localities and employers (e.g., to constrain abusive conditions in pay and housing). In the Bracero Program, the Mexican government, through its consular offices, persistently intervened to defend Mexican workers in the United States, at one point halting all contracting in the state of Texas to protest discrimination and mistreatment there (see Galarza 1964). The transnational approach would institutionalize this give-and-take. Transnational relations would be brokered through the U.S. and foreign federal governments, especially INS officers, in order to maintain a predictable negotiating structure and to overcome the problems of variable institutional capacities in different local compacts. The contrast with the present U.S. approach to international migration could hardly be greater. Currently, INS officers in international offices act as intelligence gatherers in a strictly enforcement role. Meanwhile, the consular visa officers of the Department of State, who actually do serve immigrants and travelers, have little or no relationship to domestic U.S. immigrant and host communities, so they are not a means of transnational communication and mutual regulation. In the flexible recruitment approach, the sundered domestic and international service roles would be joined together in the brokerage work of INS officers (see chapter 11 on the "new professionalism" in the INS). Also, at the present, overall U.S. government policy is to pressure sending governments to join immigration enforcement operations despite those governments' manifest reluctance to enforce U.S. immigration law against their own nationals. (This has been an important irritant in U.S. relations with Mexico, for example.) The alternative plan offers more opportunity for transnational negotiation and joint problem solving, rather than a coercive foreign policy based on the possessive and singular concept of the U.S. nation-state.

As the examples show, flexible recruitment faces substantial challenges in encompassing the variety of labor migration. Indeed, it might prove clumsy or subject to severe evasion. The fact that the present legal/illegal immigrant distinction and the kinship or occupational preferences handle the real world very inadequately is some solace, though perhaps not enough. We must be humble in arguing for a schematic alternative—a lesson that ethnography in particular teaches. Nevertheless, "numerical control," the present arrangement of migration, simply does not match reality. Actual networked migration wins out, but the hypocrisy and failure of the legal system leads to moral estrangement between hosts and migrants. We can do better.

Notes

1. Piore's model has been modified and supplemented: migratory flows also begin with geopolitics, such as U.S. intervention (e.g., Mahler 1995); the initial model was social, but not social enough, for individual migrants are part of households and other networks (Kearney 1986; Pessar 1986); and the model works in more complex ways once it is gendered (Hondagneu-Sotelo 1994). Nevertheless, Piore's basic concept is powerful and quite germane.

2. It is worth noting the modification that this makes to present U.S. employer petition policy. The current policy emphasizes certification of shortages in the domestic labor market and absence of wage undercutting (done by the Department of Labor). Alternately, it emphasizes the possession of high educational or occupational qualifications. The new scheme does not require a labor market certification, resting instead on the cost of local compacts to simulate the social wage embodied in domestic labor markets.

7

Local Compacts: Basic Format, Process, and Examples

Local compacts would emphasize democratic participation; in doing so, they would plan for collective costs of (or better said, investments in) immigration. The major participants in local compacts would include host communities of citizens (directly or through local officials), employers (as individuals or, preferably, organized groups), and existing immigrant groups organized as petitioners for conationals.[1] Their agreements would dictate how the visa sponsor (employer or immigrant organization) would pay social costs for new immigrants.[2] Local agreements would vary, but a list of reasonable provisions will give us a feel for the moral exchange at the heart of this arrangement. Sponsors would pay estimated fees for both short and long-term costs to the local compacts. The compacts would provide for adding to or recapitalizing the housing stock to support new residents. They would pay for expanding public education systems or, like housing, recapitalizing them so that they might deal successfully with the arrival of many young families. The local compact might consider supporting labor-intensive community-oriented policing (Guyot 1991). It would address the need for public clinics and emergency rooms in hospitals. The local compact should anticipate characteristic zones of tension, such as public language policy. If it did not set strict guidelines, it should at least establish public discussion and dispute resolution. Other initiatives might facilitate the evolving place of immigrants within the new society: for example, offering small loans for both immigrants and hosts, to assist the characteristic transition from jobs to small enterprises (see Mahler 1995). To make the local compact different from charity, outreach, or paternalistic "adjustment" of migrants, these fees and services ought to arise from a real engagement of sponsors, host communities, and immigrant communities in mutual-problem identification and problem solving. Paternalistic services put the recipient in a lower and passive category, and can be withdrawn; mutual agreements between equivalent parties cannot be easily broken.

The most obvious advantage of local compacts would be shifting costs from the public to migrant sponsors. This would remove a factor that significantly worsens current immigration conflict. Immigrants now use more local services (such as schools and public hospitals) than they pay in local taxes, but they are substantial net contributors of taxes to the federal government (Fix and Passel 1994:58–59, 71). (The effects on state budgets are mixed.) The local compact would increase local revenues, directed specifically at investments in social needs. If there are tax deductions for such payments, it would reduce federal and state revenues. More importantly, the compacts would add to collective goods (such as better policing or schools) at the expense of private sponsors seeking their own, narrower ends. I speculate that much of the current tension over immigration has to do with struggles over this balance between individual and collective goods, in particular goods vital to U.S. household reproduction (Carrier and Heyman 1997): house (real-estate) values (Chavez 1992), property taxes, and whose kids get what in public schools. One characteristic fear is that immigrant children hinder prosperous American children in their competitive scramble for college (author interview in San Diego County, 1992). These major, expensive consumer goods are subject not only to individual purchase but also collective political conflict. Thus they are central to current social anxieties in the United States about immigrant settlers (Chavez 1997). A mutual agreement that accounts for the needs and costs of immigrants in housing and education, and consequently increases the total supply of these fundamental goods, would go far to defuse current hostility to immigrants. Finally, the local delivery of services to immigrants, and the antecedent process of deciding what is needed, would get many persons from the host society involved in, intrigued by, and more knowledgeable of the lives of immigrants. It would promote moral commitment and interdependence.

The local compact would require participatory decision making, which is admirable but hardly simple. The local compact must start by identifying stakeholders. In this regard, the challenge would be to include people, such as African Americans, who perceive themselves as direct competitors of immigrants, as well as immigrant employers and advocates. One tool for identifying stakeholders would be a snowball sample (accumulated by using one participant to refer to addtional participants until a desired number of participants is reached) that continues until a substantial set of names are repeated; this group could then be convoked as a search conference that identifies what should happen among stakeholders in the subsequent participatory process.[3] The next step in the process would be laying out general expectations for decent community services and reasonable outcomes of immigrant settlement. This stage would be a positive negotiation (in which shared "goods" are discussed) that precedes the zero-sum negotiations over the immigration tax. This stage also could draw attention to disparities between community ideals and realities for poorer hosts. Negotiations then would shift to the specific terms of immigrant support costs. The INS would handle the application of the compact to actual immigrant sponsorship and payment. An officer of the INS also would shepherd the participatory process, thus transforming the INS in positive ways (as discussed in chapter 11). Above all, the participatory process would be the center of decision making, not just a means of providing symbolic cover and information about local opinion to the true decision makers (Ladd 1975). Participation is not just a technical mechanism here: it is the key to reversing objectification and hostility.

A major problem with calling for a participatory approach is the shallowness of participation in the current United States. To be honest and thorough, it is important to review the existing problems. In the long historical view, public participation in the United States has steadily declined because political parties are no longer what they once were: mass organizations with effective block and neighborhood clubs. Today political parties are fund-raising and spending organizations operated by a narrow segment of professionals. Other organizations, like unions, have eroded in similar ways. What has replaced the parties? First and foremost, a nonparticipatory negotiation process among experts, bureaucracies, and corporations. Public hearings that they hold consist of canned statements by public relations professionals from interest groups, and real involvement by a narrow segment of educated, upper-middle-class "citizens" (Kushma 1988; MacLennan 1994). In comparison with other advanced capitalist nations, the United States has a weak public sphere, though it also has strong individual civil and political citizenship (Turner 1990). Clearly this scenario fits with the "possessive citizenship" discussed above. Participation as a solution to polarization between host communities and new immigrants also confronts the legacy of city and county councils being used to harass and expel immigrants. (See Chavez's [1992] ethnography discussed in the "Anti-Immigrationism" section above.)

Solutions may be found in how participation is framed. Helen Ingram and Anne Schneider (1993) argue that public policies subtly but effectively dictate whose participation in society is legitimate, and whose is not. For example, laws that attribute citizenship characterize persons who are "contenders," possessors of interests admitted to the debate, as opposed to "dependents," persons who are tolerated but have no voice, and "illegitimates," persons who are actively denigrated (e.g., "illegal immigrants"). Present politics and immigration law imply that immigrants are either dependents or illegitimates, and thus worthy only of suspicion, not participation. Local meetings then are likely to exclude rather than include. The alternative immigration policy would rest on the mutual moral recognition that immigrants are legitimate precisely because they are part of the negotiation. It also would rest on the recognition that capital has obligations to local democracy, as expressed in the local investment of employment taxes. Imagine what a difference these two frames could make to immigration politics. In Chavez's San Diego case, the only subject of participation was whether to harass undocumented settlements; it was not over whether those immigrants were legally admissible, that is, legitimate (a purely nonparticipatory topic determined by federal law). Similarly, the debate did not concern the rapid real estate capitalization of what had once been a farm district. In an alternative policy, it would be necessary to admit as a first premise the existence of migrants as human beings, present in the community. Negotiations would then focus on the obligations of all parties, including farm owners and real estate developers, to the local compact. The San Diego county case suggests that a different approach *could* be ethnographically realistic. It is hard to imagine mutual participation given the historical burdens of xenophobia and apathy, but given their perils, imagine it we must.

Just as with political negotiations, ethnography helps us explore how the employment side of local compacts might work in reality. (The distinction is, of course, purely a convenience of narrative.) The Griffith and Kissam (1985) examples of farm recruitment suggest that agricultural-laboring situations could be aggregated into compacts fairly easily. Some of Griffith and Kissam's cases, notably Delmarva and Michigan, manifest precursors of local-compact participation in farmer paternalism and a moral climate among farmers about treatment of workers. (It did not always work, but it did shape most employers' behavior.) Another farm case, that of legal contract recruitment of Mexicans to work in Ontario, Canada (Colby 1997), strongly suggests that a carefully regulated recruitment system can provide positive (if paternalistic) results in housing, financial security, labor conditions and payment issues, and so forth. However, as Catherine Colby, the author of the Mexico-Ontario study, points out, the implication must be put in the context of the U.S.'s much larger, more complex, and more open migration from Mexico and other nations. (This study is discussed at greater length in chapter 12.) For instance, the vast majority of U.S. immigrants go to metropolitan areas. The issues there are more daunting than in farm labor scenarios. What do metropolitan ethnographies tell us about the politics of compacts?

Agricultural employers typically form coherent interest associations that control labor supplies. Metropolitan economic-political arenas are not as straightforward. For example, it is difficult to imagine diverse and fractured employers coming together as an interest group that undertakes self-taxation as part of the local compact. Let us explore some ethnographic cases in terms of these questions. One important metropolitan recruitment route is upper- and upper-middle class households who hire illegal and legal immigrant women (who then solicit additional kin) for domestic and nanny work. Terry Repak (1995) documents how returning expatriate Agency for International Development, State Department, and other governmental workers brought domestic workers with them from Central America, most of them sponsored under U.S. immigration laws. The pioneer immigrants initiated a chain migration that led to an extensive Central American presence in Washington, D.C. Many immigrants now own, or are employed by, ethnic businesses, but domestic work is still predominant. Given the way that upper- and upper-middle class Americans already utilize the immigration system to obtain domestic workers, it seems reasonable for metropolitan compacts to establish labor clearinghouses that attribute social costs to employers in exchange for immigration visa sponsorship. Once key migrants are part of the recruitment system, it also would be possible to require a compact-regulated sponsorship process for additional kin. The potential problem is evasion, the black-market encouragement of immigration outside compact rules, by American householders and established immigrants both; this is rendered a more distinct possibility by the dispersed and low-scale character of these labor markets.

Another metropolitan challenge is the aggregation of small businesses. Judith Goode (1994a) describes a variety of native and immigrant store owners and store workers in Philadelphia. Established native store owners offered customers close, personal attention; this helped them to retain regular customers in the face of chain-store competition. This interpersonal exchange, however, only worked with their own familiar native customers, not with new immigrants with whom they find it difficult to cultivate relations. In addition, the established store owners are aging, and their children are not fully replacing them. One response they are *not* making is developing connections to the new immigrants. Lacking any forum for relations with immigrant groups, native store owners are either hiring kin (which does not solve their long-term problems), or closing up. On the other hand, new immigrant store owners lack the language and intercultural communication skills to interact with the established customer base—they are awkward with their customers, and their customers perceive this as unfriendliness, a competitive disadvantage. The problem, of course, is that currently each store, host or immigrant, approaches its difficulties as a separate, family-based enterprise. This case shows the potential value to be gained by aggregating store owners into an association within the local compact. Immigrant store workers could be recruited to help native store owners form a moral and economic bond with immigrants; in the process, they would learn U.S. storekeeping mores vital to successful small storekeeping of their own.

These two cases offer a significant lesson. The simplest model of the local compact treats employers as a unitary class; that is an inadequate, though sometimes necessary, generalization. The realization of a new immigration policy will require creative negotiation as much with differentiated capital as with differentiated immigrants. The challenge—and potential importance—of participation is striking when we contemplate entire metropolises as "local compacts."

Metropolitan areas, such as Miami, Florida (Portes and Stepick 1993), are centers of host-immigrant conflict. Migration to Miami began as a side-effect of the U.S. government's cold war with Cuba. It thus developed without the participation of either the Anglo American establishment or the traditionally excluded African American community. Early in the Cuban immigration, reactive Miami elites pushed the federal government into resettling Cubans outside Florida; Cubans, however, rapidly returned to Miami, negating this form of local rejection. The Cuban American community independently accumulated political and economic capital, driven by hopes of return to their home country and by rejection by Anglo American institutions such as banks and the *Miami Herald*. Later, the established Cuban community bore social costs of immigration for additional Cuban emigres and Nicaraguans. African Americans, meanwhile, were excluded from power under the original Anglo American domination and the later Cuban ascendancy. Among new immigrants, Haitians entered in a notably disadvantaged legal and economic position, in part because of U.S. foreign/refugee policy but also because of the lack of a negotiating role for African Americans (their only possible supporters). The overall process resulted in exacerbating ethnic rivalries and segmentations in everyday life, such as the ones Alex Stepick and his collaborators documented in Miami workplaces (Lamphere et al. 1994; see also Grenier et al. 1992).

Let us envision the Miami experience done differently. Negotiation would begin with the idea that the Anglo American establishment could not reject Cuban refugees from the local community. In exchange, the federal government would commit itself to pay social costs to the Miami metropolitan area. (In this instance, I interpret the U.S. government to be the sponsor of refugees; see the section "An Addendum on Refugee Admissions" below.) African Americans would be major stakeholders in the compact process; while they would likely oppose new immigration, African American leaders could use the negotiations to obtain from the metropolitan area and the federal government resources as a quid pro quo. Had this happened in the past, it would have reduced the present-day alienation of key African Americans from the inner political process. One group that seems likely to be vulnerable in the compact process is Haitians, regrettably. Their local and foreign policy support seems relatively weak.

An important lesson of Miami is that the local-compact system must include major integrative institutions, for example, the *Miami Herald,* which shape metropolitan politics although they are not directly interested parties. Because the *Miami Herald* ignored immigration for so long, when it did enter the public debate it was reactive and prone to harsh ethnic objectification of host-immigrant conflict. In almost every metropolitan situation, we can identify key institutions like the *Herald.* The constructive reading of ethnographies suggests that they can be held morally responsible for their cities.

Miami and Philadelphia differ greatly. One is a growing Sunbelt city, the other a stagnant northern one. One has many immigrants, the other relatively few. Yet in both cases (Goode 1994b; Portes and Stepick 1993) key elites avoided local responsibility after firms shifted from the regional to national and global levels. Goode and Portes and Stepick show how absence of major corporate commitment to the metropolis led to political paralysis and zero-sum conflicts in the local immigration and ethnic arenas. Possibly, compacts demanding participation and local resource commitment would restore some rootedness to elite decision makers. Local compacts would not rely exclusively on elite commitments, but they would require of the upper tiers of power responsibility as well as privilege.

At this point, it is worth contemplating the approach I have taken to writing about the local compacts, for it embodies many of the strengths and weaknesses of my enterprise. I have not emphasized, in any great detail, the specific rules of how every compact would function. I have taken a different, perhaps more realistic, certainly more anthropological approach: applying the local-compact idea to actual cases, as documented by ethnographers, complete with difficulties and complications. I hope that the reader understands that local compacts would not be easy to set up, and could well go badly wrong; but then, host-immigrant relations have already gone badly wrong in situations like San Diego county or Miami. The value stance that motivates the writing is simple and hopeful; without that simplicity and hopefulness, my motivation would dissipate. My approach to the material, from processual political economy, emphasizes elements of power, interest, segmentation, and irresponsibility that make cases complicated and treacherous. There is no resolution to this tension, but I hold that the interplay between the hopeful and the critical, the platitudes and the ethnographic realities, leads us to more satisfactory social writing than the formalistic (and status-quo oriented) policy writing that pervades the immigration field.

An Addendum on Refugee Admissions

Network recruitment alone cannot handle refugee admissions, especially new or massive influxes of refugees from deteriorating situations. (Helping refugees to reunite with established compatriots in the United States would be more easily handled, through coethnic and social agency mechanisms.) For most refugees, I propose that the federal government be the "recruiter," that it at first assume social costs in local compacts, and that it integrate refugees into local compacts by connecting refugees with employers who do not have existing network relations to migrant sources.

In general, I justify the immigration alternative on the basis of its consequences. For example, increasing immigrant-host mutuality reduces harmful consequences of politicized conflict and persecution, while using a flexible recruitment system decreases harmful consequences of covert migration. Consequences, good or bad, can *persuade* us to do something (weighed against its costs, etc.), but they do not *oblige* us to do anything. For some moral issues, however, a stronger case can be made for acting, whatever the consequences and costs. These are "duties." Giving refuge from persecution (giving "asylum") is such a duty. Mark Gibney (1986) persuasively argues for two rules establishing duties, the "harm principle" (we ought to protect fellow human beings from preventable harm) and the weaker "basic rights principle" (if humans lack basic needs, we ought to give some of our available excess goods to them). We can certainly prevent significant harm to human life by giving refuge without regard to consequences.(Especially since, in the wealthy United States, we are not by any interpretation sacrificing our basic needs by a generous asylum policy.)

How, then, do we insert duties into an immigration plan otherwise composed of options, consequences, and choices? A compromise would be the federal government integrating refugees into local compacts with needs for new recruitment pools. The refugees would be directed to employers and others (e.g., a home-country organization or a coalition of churches) who seek additional recruitees. If this integration of two purposes occurs, then the local-compact system for costs and requirements would apply to the new refugee sponsors, probably with specific assistance from the federal government (representing the collective national duties in giving asylum). Including refugee issues in local participation is essential to constructing a politically viable asylum policy, since rejection of refugees is part and parcel of rejection of immigrants as a whole.

The alternative plan supposes significant changes in U.S. refugee policy: a fair application of Gibney's harm principle to admissions rather than the existing practice of unfair admissions by national origins according to foreign-policy considerations, and halting interdiction at sea that prevents persons from making claims on the United States as a nation of first asylum (e.g., not turning away Haitian boat people before asylum requests are adjudicated). Applying Gibney's harm principle will require a vast expansion of the INS asylum corps. It will require perfecting the present INS asylum—corps training in empathy and open-ended interviewing, techniques required by the circumstances of refugees (see Gilad 1990). Although any refugee with a plausible first-order claim should have a full and appealable asylum application, it is important to have large numbers of INS officers screening first-order cases from meaningless ones, since the current pattern of lengthy asylum adjudications have encouraged an industry of fraudulent asylum claims, as Sarah Mahler (1995:173–87) documents. Clearly, more needs to be said about alternative refugee policies, but the sketch here at least suggests how it might be integrated into the local-compact approach.

Notes

1. Individual immigrant households seeking to bring in network associates (their relatives, etc.) enter the process together with employers and existing immigrant groups, as described in the recruitment section.

2. Reasonably, the sponsor would count certain existing taxes (e.g., parts of state and local ones) as part of the sponsorship package, but the total bill would be greater than existing taxes.

3. I thank my colleague Kathleen Halvorsen for insights into the philosophy and concrete application of public participation.

8
Long-Term Settlement via Local Compacts

Since all immigrants would receive permanent visas under the proposal, whether they actually intend lifelong residence, all local compacts must prepare appropriate resources for enduring settlement (costs for housing, schools, etc.). Taxes collected from sponsors upon initial entrance, and not expended in a given year, would be invested for expenditure on settlement costs in subsequent years. The INS must obligate local compacts to make these long-term plans. This reflects the lesson of experience: some temporary migrants will eventually settle in the host society under any migration system. The new approach would not have temporary "guest worker" provisions, no matter how that might suit particular migrants and employers at a given time. Germany and France, for example, have had immigration plans based on employer requests to government agencies for guest workers; in Germany the stay was legally temporary and in France the assumption was that immigrants would depart although visas were lasting. In both cases, however, many migrants, their spouses, and children settled in the new nation. Neither society was then prepared to accept these settlers in the sense of a conscious political commitment of resources (Hollifield 1994; P. Martin 1994).

The United States has not had a large guest-worker program since 1965. (There are small temporary laborer provisions in current law.) However, the U.S. policy of strict numerical control of permanent visas at levels below the actual demand for U.S. entry has led to illegal migration that in some ways resembles guest working. Over time, many undocumented migrants have committed themselves to sustained residence in the United States, thus becoming covert settlers. The 1986 IRCA law permitted many undocumented settlers to legalize their residence, but that law was a one-time adjustment, while the settlement of immigrants continues unabated. Fix and Passel (1994:24) estimate that the total resident undocumented population in 1992 was about 3.2 million. Chavez (1992), in a superb ethnography of such settlers, reveals a fundamental disparity in mutual moral interchange between these people and the host nation: undocumented Mexican and Central American settlers gradually increase their commitment to the United States until they reach quite wholehearted levels, but their lack of legal personhood causes the United States, including their San Diego neighbors, to treat them as impermanent "illegals" and as people "out of place." An adequate moral and practical effort to regulate migration therefore requires an explicit political consensus that settlement is a probable outcome of all migration.

Settlers scare many Americans. Peter Brimelow (1995), a frantic and rather obvious fear monger, argues that new immigrants from Asia, Latin America, and the Caribbean will overwhelm (politically and demographically) the Euro-Americans who are the cultural bearers of the Anglophone democratic tradition. Brimelow's racism is evident, much as he denies it, in his assumption that Chinese Americans, Mexican Americans, or Trinidadian Americans are incapable of learning U.S. political traditions and sustaining democracy. After all, earlier generations of these ethnic groups successfully joined the U.S. political process, as did Jews, Scandinavians, Italians, Slavs, Lebanese, Armenians, Japanese, and all sorts of other non-Anglophones. There is, however, a more plausible and meaningful concern among many sincere Americans: that the new immigrants come from very diverse cultures and will remain just as different in the future, resulting in a fractured, indeed polarized, America.

Anthropologists ought to be heard on questions of culture; it is our chosen expertise. A mistaken notion of "culture" rests inside the fear of divisive immigrant cultures. Cultures are enormously powerful in people's behaviors and beliefs, this much is true, but they are hardly fixed in place. Cultures are adaptive and change remarkably fast. In immigration contexts, the cultural change from parents to children can be almost total. The history of the United States shows that in the vast majority of postimmigration cases change involves assimilation into the dominant American culture (see Gordon 1964). This is as true for the "new" immigrants as it was for immigrants of the turn of the century, of the 1840s, and so back in time. Assimilation, though it generally describes the American experience, is a clumsy way to show the importance of culture change; Leo Chavez's analysis of "incorporation" is more telling.

Chavez (1992) studied undocumented Latin American settlers in San Diego county, people who, because of their illegal status, have hardly been encouraged to identify with the United States; yet he clearly detected "incorporation" among them. By studying incorporation, he discovered significant moral and practical bonds with the new society, including "social incorporation," such as children born or socialized in the new land; "cultural incorporation," such as English proficiency and values of education; and "personal incorporation," the relocation to America of an emotional, meaningful sense of self-identity. Not all adult migrants went through incorporation. Many remained cyclical migrants whose incorporation is temporary and mostly economic. But Chavez found that immigrants with children who remained for long periods in the United States *did* incorporate in all these senses. More strikingly, he found that they made their offering in moral exchange to the United States. They recognized the American schools, neighborhoods, workplaces, and so forth as their primary loyalties. Can host U.S. moral actors return that recognition?

The generational transition from immigrant parents to U.S.-raised children is particularly important in incorporation. Immigrant children Americanize; the question is, in what ways and on what terms? Michael Piore's (1979) model of immigration is useful for outlining generational changes now taking place in the United States. According to the model, most adult immigrants will incorporate relatively little because they migrate, take work, and adopt other roles based largely on their needs in the social structure of the nation of origin. A Mexican small landowner, then, accepts low status and dead-end work as a garden laborer or a janitor. Young people who grow up in the United States, however, internalize its hierarchy of social values—and rightly so, if we emphasize assimilation and the plasticity of culture. They undergo years of public schooling, which ostensibly point them at jobs requiring educational credentials, bureaucratic finesse, or advanced blue collar skills. We value these jobs, and so do the sons and daughters of the immigrant garden laborers and the janitors. The United States, however, does not consistently deliver to young people the education and the labor market paths corresponding to this profound "Americanness" (e.g., Finnegan 1996; Griffith and Kissam 1995: ch. 4). At times, we do a good job, but we could do better. The two greatest barriers may be minority group alienation from stratifying, factory-model public education (Foley 1990; Ogbu 1987), and rigidly segmented, stagnant, or declining labor markets that provide insufficient opportunities for job entry and mobility. Really, these concerns hold true for all young people, not just for immigrant children. An excellent example of these processes can be found in Philippe Bourgois's account of young Puerto Rican men in New York's changing economy, "from jíbaro [rustic] to crack dealer" (1995a, 1995b). I wonder, only slightly sarcastically, whether immigration to the United States ought to be curtailed, not because immigrants are bad for the United States, but because the United States is bad for the immigrants—especially for their children.

This monograph, however, can hardly address either education or labor markets, beyond a modest contribution made by local compacts. The compact would increase collective (shared) goods that help the younger generation, such as housing, schooling, and community policing.

The compact taxation arrangement would also be helpful in redressing the uneven fiscal burden of providing services to heavy immigrant areas, since by taxing petitioners (e.g., employers), it makes immigrants into a fiscal resource as well as a regional burden. (See chapter 8 on using taxation to even out the currently distorted fiscal impacts of immigration.) By inculcating values of tolerance, as well as specific opportunities for mutual involvement, it might bring older and long-assimilated Americans to see the worth of the children of immigrants. This would be helpful in building up long-term support for costly collective goods such as public education. One thing is certain: both practical and moral support could make a meaningful difference to immigrant families negotiating the transitions of incorporation into U.S. life.[1]

Janet Benson's (1994) ethnography of Southeast Asian refugee families working in midwestern packinghouses demonstrates the damaging effects of lack of support, and indicates what difference moral and practical support could make. The refugees have admirable educational goals for their children. At great cost they invest their savings and emotional capital in their children's future. Someone who feared that new immigrants do not want to incorporate into U.S. life would do well to read Benson's chapter. Tragically, however, she shows that pressures on household economies, felt especially by women, obstruct these long-term goals in favor of short-term survival. The effects of packinghouse work and tight budgets include forced overtime and jobs pressed on mothers by the need to earn money to meet rents. They take in boarders, also to pay for housing, causing chaotic, sometimes threatening household environments. They also neglect health problems of both parents and children because of lack of income and health insurance. A supportive, housing, and service-providing local compact could relieve these pressures, thereby liberating people's powerful ambition for their children. Can this be achieved? It would take a greater moral commitment from the U.S. public.

The present political climate polarizes hosts and immigrants. In this situation, immigrant families and children become political "enemies" of American nationalists, rather than bearers of a shared future. Proposition 187 appealed to voters' desire to punish undocumented immigrants by taking away their schooling and medical care, just as the 1996 immigration and welfare laws take away household support (medicaid, food stamps, and supplemental security income) from legal immigrants. Benson's ethnography tells us that taking away medical assistance and income from disabled or elderly household members will hurt the persistence in school of immigrant children; it also sends the message that they are illegitimate students. A more destructive future for American children can hardly be imagined. Therefore, it is essential that we do the following things: (1) restore social benefits to all legal immigrants; (2) make immigrants legal rather than illegal, with complete legitimacy in social distributions; and (3) add to the pool of collective goods dedicated to the next generation of host and immigrant children. Even more important than these recommendations about benefits, we must establish a moral commitment of host Americans to the immigrant children, a commitment that would recognize them as fellow, deserving members of society, in whose success we all share.

Notes

1. Recent research has shown that different immigrants come to the United States with different amounts of education, skills, and so on, and enter different labor markets (see Edmonston and Passel 1994). For these reasons, non-Cuban Latino immigrants do not move upward from poverty as quickly as non-Latinos. Some immigration policy advocates, like George Borjas (1990), argue that the United States should design an occupational (and tacitly, ethnically restrictive) immigration policy to get immigrants with labor-market trajectories most suited to a high-education United States. It would be incorrect to ignore the particular difficulty of long-term poverty and declining markets for laboring Latinos. Yet Borjas's solution has a naive faith in numerical control—it assumes that we can tailor immigrant entry to get certain qualities—that has simply proven ineffectual; in fact, the United States offers jobs, lots of them, for unskilled laboring Mexicans, but does not match that attraction factor with a commitment to long-term inclusion. For example, even as unskilled jobs stagnate, the United States is short of blue collar workers with a post–high school education (community college or bachelor of engineering technology degree) needed for high-paying jobs in advanced manufacturing. The answer is to recognize that poor Latinos and many others in the United States face a variety of potential futures depending on the commitment of U.S. society to their development. The future does not rest *only* in their essential qualities. Jeffrey Passel and his colleagues review "positive" (assimilative or adjustment-oriented) immigration policies at federal and state levels, and advocate their greater use as a tool of U.S. migration policy (Edmonston and Passel 1994; Fix and Passel 1994).

9
Border Control in a New Immigration Policy

The local-compact policy would free the United States from its present treadmill of escalating border patrolling; it offers a positive, new vision of America's borders. In recent years, the United States has rapidly escalated police and military force at the Mexican border (Barry et al. 1994; Dunn 1996; Heyman, n.d.[b]). In 1996, Congress authorized doubling the Border Patrol from 5,000 to 10,000 officers in the period 1997–2002. Massive iron plates line the 14 miles of the San Diego border from the Pacific Ocean to the Otay Mountain foothills; the 1996 legislation authorizes making that wall three layers deep. Similar walls have been built at high crossing zones throughout the border. Less dramatically, but perhaps more importantly, the INS now relies on massed Border Patrol operations, using hundreds to thousands of officers, to control the border. A skeptical reader might reply that "of course, the entrants are illegal, and walls and massed operations are rational responses to extensive law-breaking." In fact, these law enforcement approaches have so far not been effective, and they have undesirable consequences for the development of the U.S.-Mexico borderlands. While the latter is my main concern, and I think it an important one, it merits briefly reviewing the evidence on the effectiveness of massive control operations. Frank Bean and his colleagues, looking at Operation Hold-the-Line in El Paso, found that it was locally successful in reducing illegal border crossings. However, the primary undocumented immigrant stream, that of migrants making the long-distance journey from the interior of Mexico to the interior of the United States, was not prevented from entering but was displaced to other areas of the border (Bean et al. 1994). Other evidence suggests that undocumented immigration rates are more strongly affected by the state of the Mexican economy than by U.S. spending on enforcement; policing the boundary simply raises the payoff for smugglers (see Singer and Massey 1997). Border Patrolling may not work well, but is there a better way to control the border? I think that there is.

To move toward an alternative on the border, it will first be necessary to relieve the build-up of political pressure. This pressure comes from the internal politics of anti-immigrationism, not from the actual flow of undocumented entrants (which, at most, affects some tactical allocations by the INS). Thus I will suggest that improving host-immigrant relations far from the boundary and altering the politics of citizenship would relieve the political pressure to escalate force at the border. Second, an alternative immigration policy would need systems for monitoring and controlling entry at the border and at other ports of entry (airports, etc.). I do not propose open borders, but rather to use the boundary as a registration point for the regulation of flows. Regulation would begin with entry into the country and culminate with arrival in a local compact. Finally, I will argue that the current escalation of the border region into a police zone harms its long-term development. Ending the harm done by the destructive cycle of smuggling and policing to the U.S.-Mexico border region justifies abandoning the present approach to law enforcement there.

The United States escalates force at the boundary because of the symbolic displacement of interior tensions toward the national margin. A counterargument is to view U.S. policy as genuinely motivated by its overt goal, halting illegal migration. It is very difficult to disprove this sort of "face-value" hypothesis, since even if we consider the evidence that it does not work, it could be a misguided but sincere policy. The evidence I cite above shows that it has not yet worked. Additionally, a very convincing case *can* be made for the hidden motivation hypothesis.

As we saw above, the majority of people in polls would restrict immigration when immigrants are considered at a distance. What is more important, they assume that, contrary to reality, most immigrants are illegal. "Illegality" in this case is a symbol, not just a lacuna of information. Symbolic fears surrounding immigration ineluctably lead to escalation at the Mexican border (as documented in Rodriguez 1997). As recited earlier, in the aftermath of the *state* of California vote in favor of Proposition 187, political leaders in both major parties emphasized border patrolling, a *federal* duty. At a regional level, too, conflict is displaced and projected onto the border. During the early 1980s, the *Miami Herald* advocated "rigid" border control, among other immigration measures (Portes and Stepick 1993:173), although Miami is far from the Mexican boundary and has few land border-crossing immigrant streams (with the exception of late 1980s Nicaraguans). Local participation that lead to direct contact between hosts and immigrants would diminish the outward projection of fear and its wishful resolution in policing at a distance. Recall the evidence that people, when faced with actual immigrant profiles, reacted more favorably to immigration than when they were just provided the term "illegal immigration." Relaxing the symbolic "border" will make possible a more adequate real border policy.[1]

In a flexible immigration system, the border would become a clearinghouse rather than a place of enforcement. The INS currently inspects nonimmigrants (e.g., tourists, students) and immigrants alike at ports of entry; they review paperwork prepared by the Department of State that gives the person a visa, and inspect entrants for excludable traits (such as past felonies), which might result in denial of entry.[2] The INS could easily expand this visa-checking role into its principal enforcement role on the border. A person within a local compact that petitioned for an immigrant would enter that request to the INS local area coordinator; then, the coordinator would transmit the approved petition to an issuer of visas (either the INS or the State Department, as in the present system). Exclusions could be enforced at the issuance of the visa and at the border, as they are done now. (I leave aside here the important, but lateral topic of the reform of exclusion categories.) The immigrant would present the visa at the border, where the INS inspector would review the database of immigration petitions. The INS might also issue the visa at the port of entry itself in cases where the database showed the approval of the petition.

The alternative plan would strengthen the INS's existing role as facilitator of transactions and diminish its role as enforcer. We could expect a very large and labor-intensive INS at the border—but one with a very different mission. Undoubtedly, many hopeful immigrants would arrive at the border with confused and incomplete petitions, or no petition at all, simply the hope of finding a job or a relative. Meanwhile, some compacts might have open petitions for day laborers. The INS officer would broker these arrangements. The officer would, of course, require time (even in a computer-networked era) to clear such petitions with local compacts. In such cases, a novel duty of the INS would be providing humane shelter for waiting periods—as opposed to present-day enforcement where the INS invests resources in detention, a punitive form of shelter. With all this said, however, we can expect many persons to cross the border illegally to avoid a long wait, or with no intention of following the slow visa process.

Surprisingly, the new policy would tolerate extralegal crossing; it would not be the focus of border law enforcement. (The INS may retain some capacity to discourage mass evasive crossing by intermittent sweeps to bring persons to ports of entry, where they enter the legal queue.) There would continue to be patrolling to screen for safety, to discourage bandits who victimize migrants, and to rescue border crossers who are in danger. How can I advocate abandoning border enforcement? Let me reply with a further question: if immigrants crossed the boundary illegally, where would they go? They either would have a specific destination in mind, or would be working on a loose, improvised plan. In either case, they would end in a local compact area. The compact would have vast power, since it would control access to all the valued resources: jobs, help with housing, and so on. Without these resources, extralegal immigrants would gradually be discouraged, and this information would arrive back at the starting point to "enforce" the formal paths and channels.

There undoubtedly would be considerable seepage and exploration by undocumented immigrants, even under the local-compact system; there is reason to expect, however, that some compacts could offer on-the-spot visas to undocumented immigrants for peak workforces (as discussed in the section on recruitment, above). The local INS coordinator could adjust the immigrants' statuses. A more elaborate clearinghouse network also could transfer such "seeping migrants" to compacts that do have open demands. However, we could not avoid continuing to give INS officers the ultimate power to enforce the limits set in local compacts by arresting undocumented entrants and offering them voluntary departure (leaving the United States without a formal deportation hearing and without a legal record). Usually, this arrest would not take place at the border but at the compact area itself. The point is that many options exist before enforcement lands on the shoulders of the undocumented immigrant. By contrast, in the present system the INS either makes direct arrests for voluntary departure with no meaningful options for either agent or migrant, or (in a much smaller number of cases) the options come into play only through postarrest immigration court and appeals (see Harwood 1986b), a harsh and inefficient way of delivering discretion.

Entry at nonborder sites, especially airports, could be handled readily. There, immigrants would openly and willfully enter bureaucratic control in the form of the passenger manifest. At that time, petitioned immigrants would be accepted and nonpetitioned ones rejected. This is similar to current practice; the United States requires proper visas before anyone can board flights to the United States, let alone enter the nation. Of course, a few persons secure tickets to the United States with a nonimmigrant visa, destroy the visa in mid-flight, and claim asylum upon landing (in which instance they are detained until their case is adjudicated). The United States now tries to address this through rapid first-contact review of asylum requests. (Persons with plausible cases are allowed to enter the nation, while final decisions are made in immigration court.) A much larger number of people enter the United States on a nonimmigrant visa (student, tourist, and so on) and then overstay their visas, becoming undocumented immigrants. There is virtually no control over this form of illegal migration to the United States at the present, although it may account for just under half the undocumented immigrants in the United States.[3] The power of the local compact to deny jobs and social distributions would discourage visa overstays. Another enforcement issue, border control along coastlines such as Florida, would be handled in the same way as the land-border situation described above, with appropriate asylum review procedures mixed in. As we survey these various scenarios, we encounter complexity in regulating entry and movement. This is to be expected, and is less a flaw of the alternative than it is a reflection of realistic subtlety and flexibility in immigration processes.

Reforming the goals of immigration law enforcement at the southern boundary will allow a healthy future for the social development of the Mexico-U.S. border. What are borders? The answer may seem obvious, but only at the surface. Of course, every border, strictly defined (see Alvarez 1995), is the dividing line between two nation-states, or similar political entities. Yet such a starting point characterizes only the formal aspects of a border, not the historical society that grows up in that setting. Yet the size of United States and Mexican cities along the boundary—San Diego, Tijuana, El Paso, Ciudad Juarez, Brownsville, Matamoros, and so on—should impress on us the importance of border society to both nations. I have characterized the Mexican border through four perspectives (Heyman 1994). The border is an *image* of disorder and change in U.S. society generally, as we have seen above. In local reality, interplay between force-backed *state regulators* (e.g., the INS and U.S. Customs) and value-seeking *transactors* (ranging from smugglers to American multinationals operating factories in border Mexico) makes and remakes the *on-the-ground border*. Amid these processes dwell the *people* of the border, some of them officers of the two nation-states, others of them commuting workers, factory managers, smugglers, and transactors of various sorts. It is with these people that we should be concerned.

Above, I described the rapid growth of the INS and the military at the Mexican border, but I did not then discuss the counterprocess: an increase in alien smuggling. It seems counterintuitive that adding law enforcement should increase rather than repress crime, but this is true for smuggling. Many migrants from Mexico, especially veteran ones, and a smaller proportion of migrants from Central America, cross the border by themselves, through well-known routes (Chavez et al. 1990). When the Border Patrol cuts the main, easy, and obvious routes, however, and increases the overall chance of being arrested, the work of the smuggler becomes more valuable to migrants. For example, undocumented immigrants have been displaced from the low canyons and hills of far western San Diego county to the more dangerous and less familiar Otay mountains to the east. Substantial journalistic and scholarly evidence indicates that the recent rise in concentrated Border Patrol force has lead to a commensurate rise in the use of, and the prices charged by, smugglers (Dillon 1996; Graham 1996; Rotella 1995; Singer and Massey 1997).

Smuggling, in turn, engenders a complicated shadow world of bosses, guides, drivers, bosses, money handlers, safe houses, informants, INS investigators, double operators, and so forth. No published source adequately penetrates this world, but see descriptions in Conover (1987). My incomplete knowledge derives from fieldwork with INS agents, and before that, subtle clues and gossip garnered during just under two years' residence in a pair of Mexican-U.S. border towns. The relevant question is, do Americans want this shadow world to shape the borderlands? It will if we allow rigid state power and illegal value-seeking transactors to dominate the region.

The people of the Mexican border are extraordinary. Carlos Vélez-Ibañez (1996) and Oscar Martínez (1994) describe the rich cultural skills of bilingual, binational, bicultural border people. There are many roles for the skillful biculturalist: maquiladora (binational factory) manager, educator, customs broker, dual-community civic activist, and so on. Smuggling and illegal transactions between two nations, however, draw the attention, energy, and knowledge of many border biculturalists. (See, for example, the oral history of Francisco Hidalgo, in Martínez 1994:175–181, 253–260.) Portes and Stepick (1993) describe the considerable advantages provided to Miami by Cuban American biculturalists, who have become significant brokers for the United States throughout Latin America. The way in which the larger United States treated Miami allowed it to transcend its considerable involvement in smuggling and money laundering. The Mexican border, too, could become a significant brokerage point with Mexico; whatever one thinks of NAFTA and the maquiladoras, the reality is that there are great advantages for playing (or translating extralegal capital into) a legitimate brokerage role and great penalties (in arrest rates and recidivism, in social immobility, loss of political power, etc.) for playing an *illegal* role. The U.S. borderlands are an important region of the nation, though outsiders are only gradually discovering this. Do we, and most importantly, border people themselves want a future shaped around an underworld, with biculturalists rewarded for their skill in smuggling and its outlying enterprises, while agencies of the U.S. state, the INS, Customs, DEA, and so forth occupy the U.S. side like a clumsy foreign army? Is this path of human development too great a price to pay for an immigration policy whose merits are debatable anyway?[4] We *can* envision a different border.

Notes

1. Importantly, relaxing the projection of symbolic fear onto the border frees the INS and U.S. border policy makers from incentives that reward escalation of

policing. I have argued elsewhere that internal U.S. symbolic politics is a political resource for the INS, especially the Border Patrol, to increase the size of its budget and the force of its policing; I also argue that the failure of numerical control and immigration policy generally causes loss of credibility for the U.S. state elite, to which they react by escalation of force (Heyman n.d.[b]). It might be proposed, however, that a purely local and symbolic-emotional resolution of tension cannot redirect the large-scale tendency of the modern U.S. state, its managers and its technologies, toward militarization. To this useful, if gloomy, argument, the only hopeful reply is that if we do take the centralization of U.S. power seriously, we ought to curb any wellsprings of its increase.

2. The State Department provides nonimmigrant visas in most cases from outside the United States, though inside the United States the INS renews such visas. The INS adjudicates immigrant petitions (basic legal requirements compared with documentation), but the Department of State issues the immigrant visa for persons outside the United States; the INS issues immigrant visas only in the case of adjustment of status inside the United States from nonimmigrant or temporary resident status. The INS can refuse admission on entry to a person bearing an approved immigrant visa, though this is rare.

3. Fix and Passel (1994:24) estimate that 62 percent of undocumented immigrants come from Mexico, the Caribbean, and Central America, and 38 percent come from elsewhere. It is likely that most of these 38 percent are nonborder immigrants (visa overstays). In addition, Caribbean and some Central American immigrants may not be border crossers, but Fix and Passel do not break down the categories extensively by nationality.

4. The local-compact system, the emphasis on recruitment rather than numerical control, and especially the relaxed, regulatory handling of undocumented immigration, would reduce the cycle of policing and migrant smuggling. It could not address another focus of illegality at the border, which is narcotics smuggling and law enforcement. Clearly, we have to think about somewhat similar approaches to drug law reform in the United States (see Benjamin and Miller 1991 and Bertram et al. 1996), but that is a different subject than the one at hand.

10
A New Policy, A New INS

An alternative immigration system would require a large organization to guide and rationalize the movement of migrants—perhaps as many officers as the ten thousand envisioned for the Border Patrol in the 1996 immigration act. These INS officers, however, would work with the flow of immigration, rather than against it. Flexible migrant movement and placement would require the retrieval and transmission of large volumes of information about individuals and households, made possible by the arrival of distributed and networked computing. (I will raise questions about the role of surveillance and control in a later chapter.) Thus the new immigration proposal, like any serious alternative, demands that scholars contemplate the design of governmental power. What would a new INS look like? Diagnosing the characteristics of the present Immigration Service will help us answer this.

Radical critiques of the status quo often ignore the work done by civil servants, emphasizing instead the deeper structures of their actions and policies as a whole. The unstated assumption is that if the root causes are addressed, the bureaucrats will follow. On the other hand, the "moral witness" genre often targets the specific misdeeds and organizational malfeasance of bureaucrats (e.g., the human rights abuse charges leveled at the INS, cited below). The criticisms should be united: bureaucratic misbehavior is promoted by fundamental disorders. Conversely, a positive engaged social science must face the reality of civil servants and state power. As Carol MacLennan (1988) argues, civil servants are central to the democratic administration of government. The INS seems particularly unpromising for a participatory immigration system because of its current investment in massive law enforcement and its flaws as an organization. We might dismiss the very thought of positive immigration officers. Michael Lipsky (1980), however, shows that "street-level bureaucrats" make or break the possibility of change because they deliver the service and apply the policy. In this role the street-level bureaucrat is not an obstacle but a resource for activating real change. Lipsky's approach is "the new professionalism," a positive set of ideals, duties, and resources to reshape the work lives of the civil servants. With this in mind, I start by taking apart the INS work experience and organizational process (e.g., positive and negative feedbacks about discretionary job choices). I then envision how the INS could be put back together with the INS officer as a responsible, positive actor at the center.

Although we associate the INS with its branch, the Border Patrol, it is, of course, a complex organization with a variety of job duties. Many INS officers "serve" legal entry and migration, as opposed to enforcing migration restriction. On the whole, though, present INS work involves *guarding a restricted value:* secure, legal admission to the United States. This design of INS duties is consistent with possessive citizenship. INS adjudicators review the legal documentation for petitioners for admission or adjustment to permanent legal immigrant status. They often emphasize weeding out fraudulent and inappropriate applications. They do not take the particular immigrant's circumstances, and try to match that with an available legal entry opportunity—a revealing counterfactual proposition. INS inspectors review persons entering the United States through official ports, and pass through the citizens, permanent residents, and legal temporary visitors. Although the INS classifies them as service officers rather than enforcement officers, the character of the "service" provided is restrictive. INS inspectors I interviewed described breaking fraudulent claims to U.S. citizenship (as a way to enter) as the most satisfying aspect of their job (Heyman 1995:271–273). INS Investigators, who are plainclothes police operating in the interior of the nation, and uniformed Border Patrol officers, who enforce immigration laws at the boundary or along highways, are unambiguously representatives of the restrictive side of the law. My own fieldwork, and the observations of other scholars (e.g., Juffras 1991:92), converge in saying that an "enforcement bias" pervades the INS.

The working INS officer receives two kinds of feedback from the larger society. She or he obtains a broad ideological message, whose basic content I have outlined above: beleaguered nationalism, with a strong emphasis on the division between citizen and outsider, and, especially now, very hostile ideas about undocumented immigrants. One feature of the broad ideologization of the job is that even the sympathetic INS officer understands immigration as a process of outsiders penetrating the United States, rather than a process made possible by domestic actors. Some perceptive officers do understand and articulate these connections, but such understandings do little but frustrate them, for they are inconsistent with the routine character of their jobs (see Heyman 1995).

On a task-by-task basis, the INS officer receives narrower feedback. The Administrative Procedures Act (APA), which requires publication and comment on draft regulations, is the bulwark of citizen participation in U.S. federal rule making. In the immigration sphere, the APA characteristically obtains feedback from the American Immigration Lawyers

Association, whose focal concern is business petitions for permanent and temporary immigrants, from specific employers such as the hospital industry, who petition for many immigrants, and from the airlines, who bear certain burdens in terms of passenger visas and inspections. Thus feedback does not come from the vast majority of interested parties in immigration, be they U.S. communities, established immigrant networks, employers of many documented or undocumented immigrants, or prospective entrants. Also, the APA injects participation only at the point of rule making. It does not do so for the discretionary decisions made in daily INS work. At that level, feedback includes moral witness critics (if they penetrate the local media), local phone calls to the INS (which usually provide information aimed at the arrest of individuals), and calls from congressional offices (which scare INS officers, so they protect themselves by not deviating from the narrow language of the law and exercising very limited discretion; see Gilboy 1992). Appeals and precedent decisions in the immigration court system are a final form of feedback, which is very unusual for individual officers (if important to the INS and the law as a whole, especially for legal admissions and asylum). As a feedback mechanism legal appeals are indirect, very slow, and restricted to novel or disputed legal terrains, not to "normal" (set-in-place) processes. Appeals also depend on the presence of business-oriented immigration lawyers or the small band of moral advocates.

When we speak about feedback, we are really discussing the street-level bureaucrat's experience of "participation." In this sense, narrow groups currently participate in important INS decisions about admitting or regulating specific immigrants or well-defined immigrant streams. For example, phone calls complaining about immigrants and seeking their arrest are the main way INS officers perceive the "opinion" of the local community. As a whole, U.S. society participates in the INS through abstract sets of ideological mandates, supported by generous budgets, to protect restricted citizenship against outsiders.[1]

Given the feedback about guarding citizenship, INS officers emphasize enforcing the law against individual violators rather than intervening in the immigration-using processes of U.S. society. We have already discussed the weak enforcement of the laws forbidding employment of undocumented immigrants, and the way that this debility shelters business ideology and interests in the United States. One can move through INS operations and find a consistent pattern: little patches of systemic enforcement surrounded by vast fields of individual inspection, adjudication, and arrest. The emphasis on the individual violator rather than the social process of migration, in turn, limits the true capabilities of INS workers. They are fairly competent at deciding the answer to restricted legal questions—for example, does this person in our hands have a defined right to be in the United States?—unless the area of the law is complex and discretionary, such as asylum. Consistent with this limited concept of the task, street-level INS officers are competent at basic identification; they become knowledgeable about typical immigrant behaviors, backgrounds, and claims, but the nature of their knowledge is routine and one-dimensional (Heyman 1995). INS officers do commit legal and human rights abuses on occasion; the rate of abuse versus nonabuse is unknown, but abuses' occurrence is documented (American Friends Service Committee 1990, 1992; Americas Watch 1992, 1993, 1995; Petition 1992).

The organization also has substantial managerial problems. It is notorious for logistical and budgetary chaos, and chronic corruption (Brinkley 1994). More important, the INS is characterized by massive "indifference," as Michael Herzfeld (1992) terms the familiar bureaucratic attitudes of impersonality and rudeness. One has only to observe the incredibly overcrowded service offices in INS districts. When I observed such an office in a large western city, people started waiting at seven in the morning, and stayed all day, in order to do only part of a lengthy sequence of forms and interviews. Indifference and inefficiency arise partly from the overwhelming workload in the Service. Lack of meaningful feedback from immigrants leads to a lack of responsiveness to them, as does the larger message that immigrants are low priorities in U.S. society. Feedback from the local host community, consisting mostly of enforcement tips, does not thereby redress the shortage of resources and indifference to service roles in the INS. Finally, as Herzfeld points out, bureaucratic flexibility and creativity is offered to familiars, and indifference practiced on symbolic outsiders. The INS role as guardian of a restricted value, citizenship, implies indifference to noncitizens. In the broader political arena, also, the shabby treatment of the INS (especially its routine service and inspection duties, as opposed to border patrolling) is explained by the low valuation of immigrants. The INS ranks low in power and prestige in the Department of Justice, it has a reputation for losing competent civil servants to better agencies, and officers often experience their work not as autonomous professional duties but as a set of monitored, routine tasks. INS officers do get the message.

To support these analyses, and demonstrate how they fit together in a work process, let me describe observations I made during my fieldwork with the INS in 1992. I accompanied INS investigators in a sequence of employment sanctions inspections. We first visited a Mexican bakery, where an undocumented young man was arrested by one agent as he ran out of the back door. Meanwhile, inside the bakery, the other officer gathered from the bakery owner the employment paperwork that should have recorded the documentation required for all hirings in the United States. The INS officers drove the young man to his mothers' house, where he told her that he had been arrested, and he gathered papers having to do with his legal position. He admitted that he was in the United States illegally, but told the investigators that he was within six months of receiving his immigrant visa; he was living with his legal resident mother and siblings in the United States while waiting for his number to come up in the slow visa queue. The investigators, after looking at his papers, did not question his story, but were uninterested in it (since he did not have an actual legal right at that time to reside in the United States); when they did question the young man, it was to ascertain that the baker had indeed known that he was undocumented when he was hired. That was an enforceable crime committed by the baker. Talking with the young man, I found out that he was going to ask to go before an immigration judge, in order to ask for a delay of deportation until his legal visa came through. At the time, this was a sensible approach. Since the 1996 Immigration Act, however, in such a situation he would not be allowed to legally immigrate for ten years.

We made a number of other stops that day, including looking for an allegedly illegal Canadian; the tip had come to the INS because he was beating his girlfriend. Unfortunately, he had left town. The investigators were enthusiastic about this case, because they felt that the immigrant was a "bad guy" (that is, morally worse than just an illegal immigrant); it was also proof that they did not target just Hispanics in this large southwestern city. At the end of the day, talking with the two investigators, one complained energetically and earnestly that employer sanctions were a waste of time, because all they ever busted were "little ethnic businesses" (like the Mexican bakery), hurting their survival, while the loopholes in the law protected large employers. He knew, well enough, that this was a gross generalization, but it did bear some truth about the flaws of the IRCA law (see chapter 5), and, more importantly, it was his own reflection on the limitations of his job.

What are we to make of this story? The two investigators had college educations and lengthy experience in multiple branches of the INS; they were as well-suited to be sophisticated professionals as anyone I interviewed in the Service. They understood the limitations of their jobs, and perhaps even more important, had an inkling of the social process of migration, as demonstrated by the "little ethnic businesses" discussion. Yet, in the current law, they could not work *with* the bakery owner, only charge him with a serious violation of the law. Likewise, they were indifferent to the young illegal immigrant, despite his pending visa—this was a matter for an immigration judge to decide, weeks or months down the line. In the flexible recruitment system, they could have used their power with the bakery owner to legalize the young immigrant in exchange for compact payments. Giving INS officers the legal and political discretion to arrange immigration petitions would be key.

How would change in the basic premises and characteristics of work alter the behavior of INS officers? First, the participatory system aims for meaningful feedback from local compacts of immigrants and hosts. It would require the INS officer to work with immigrants and hosts in complex and sustained ways on migrant recruitment chains and local-compact rules. It would define local citizens and immigrants as legitimate participators. It would thereby promote bureaucratic responsiveness rather than indifference to outsiders. Second, it is premised on the idea that entry to the United States is not a singular, precious good bestowed by legal admission. Legal admission would be a long-term process from before entry (setting goals and costs), through actual petition and first admission, then many job and location transfers, to final settlement. This implies, third, that INS work would be intricate and complex, involving negotiations and adjustments, rather than simple determinations of law. Officers would rise to the level of that work. Finally, the new system would undermine the enforcement bias of the INS. Since immigration enforcement would consist of adjustment or relocation of erstwhile migrants to the terms of specific compacts, even enforcement would have a service-to-persons component.[2]

These postulations might appear fanciful. Can INS officers be trusted to change radically their orientation? Lipsky's (1980) comprehensive study of street-level bureaucrats provides some hope for an affirmative response. After reviewing the typical approaches to reforming organizations, which involve increasing control and constraint on civil servants in order to force reforms, Lipsky concludes that such approaches are unlikely to succeed. He shows that street-level bureaucrats will always have choices and areas of discretion. Inevitably, they will evade top-down reforms in favor of their own routines that make their overwhelming work easier. Instead, Lipsky proposes a different type of reform: that such workers grow into "new professionals." New professionalism includes older ideals of professionalism, such as education, social respect, and a high degree of work autonomy directed through a strong ethic of service. Professional work integrates multiple functions and demands creativity rather than routinization. To this, *new* professionals will add strong peer support and evaluation (with ample client feedback on job performance): two qualities in tension, but fruitful in combination. Of course, Lipsky points out that improving professionals requires generous resources to allow job advancement and reward, and to reduce caseload pressures (numbers of complex tasks in a given period). The latter, in turn, would facilitate creativity and flexibility in professional work. MacLennan (1988) suggests that civil servants who participate in the key decisions governing their own daily work process develop the security and autonomy that would allow them to become more open to the participation of larger society. The new professional solution to the reform of public services thus uses rather than fights against the street-level workers' influence over policy.

Would not this scenario lead to professionals run amok, unconstrained powerholders dictating their social conceptions on other people's lives? The new immigration professionals would be checked within a strong local political process. They would formulate and maintain a compact of local opinions and interests, involving many different reference groups and voices. Importantly, the immigrants themselves would not be just the object of work, but a valued constituency, "contenders," not "dependents" (legal immigrants) or "illegitimates" (illegal immigrants) to use Ingram and Schneider's terms (1993). New Americans would be an accepted source of feedback for the immigration manager, both through their voice in compacts and their much greater range of legal choices than in current immigration law. In this way, the conditions would be met for Lipsky's new professionalism and for realistic democratic participation in the immigration bureaucracy.

The new immigration policy would have several key functional positions. Local immigration managers would guide the negotiation and evolution of the local compact. They would also administer its implementation, such as matching particular immigrant network petitioners with specific employers who would undertake the conditions and payments required for sponsorship. Obviously, in large settings, this would require an entire office of professionals. The important point is that immigration officers would participate in the entire sequence of policy and operations, rather than enforcing, rigidly and literally, an already-written set of laws and regulations. The handling of particular cases would vary as the immigrant networks, employers, and other sponsors do, so that the work would be creative and flexible. Border entrance inspectors would also be important, with creativity coming in the exploration of open compact positions throughout the nation for speculative migrants. In essence, the first role would be political negotiator and case manager; the second would be market broker. The nature of the work would contribute to professionalism; it would involve complicated applications of many different elements of law and regulations rather than assignment to isolated functions (inspector, adjudicator, investigator, etc.).

Notably, altering INS work would change how immigration officers view immigrants. Officers often know quite a lot about immigrants. Their job, however, affects the character of that knowledge: frequently, it consists of one-dimensional plausible stories about typical immigrant behaviors, such as how they use legitimate and nonlegitimate documentation, that respond to certain narrow task requirements (Harwood 1986; Heyman 1995). If the tasks become multifunctional, and if the interaction with the immigrants involves not just limited encounters but gathering information about complex events and alternatives in people's lives, then the immigration officer's understanding of, and behavior toward, migrants would necessarily change. INS negotiation work would lead to understanding migration as connections and constituencies, while undercutting the older INS model of immigration as isolated individuals in the right or wrong. This would make immigrant opinions more salient to INS officers, decrease indifference, and possibly reduce the misinterpretations and overreactions that lead to human rights abuses.

In overview, then, I envision improving the INS in the following ways. Democratic participation would direct immigration work in a localistic and concrete fashion, rather than in a delocalized manner that shapes the INS by giving it ideological and budgetary mandates for migration restriction. The domain of democratic input into the INS would expand to include immigrants themselves. There would be politicized demands to increase resources for the INS, just as in the present, but they would not aim at escalating force but at improving the ability of local migration managers to solve pressing problems. The nature of INS work, its creativity and professionalism, the changed meaning of "immigrant," and the reduction of national-level ideologies of possessive citizenship, would result in significant reduction of "indifference."

However, can the current INS make this change? Can it sustain the alternative immigration policy? There are many important barriers, including the ingrained work routines learned with considerable effort by present INS workers, which orient them to view immigrants not as cooperators in an enterprise, but as a deft and resistant population insinuating themselves into the United States. Another difficulty lies in the existing enforcement orientation of the INS; for example, if we look at INS career paths (Heyman 1995), we see that the vast majority of workers start in either the Border Patrol or Inspections, jobs consisting of routine mass-control tasks. Above all, Lipsky links the prospects for new professionalism to strong social movements from below, which not only create the political conditions for generous organizational reforms, but also keep autonomous officers in check. In the U.S. context, however, the most effective social movement has been anti-immigrationism, and while immigrant and immigrant-networked community movements exist (e.g., Acuña 1984: 236, 251), they are scattered and not strong. At this point, the alternative proposal could go off course, for without an effective immigrant movement, employers and other unchecked local interests might capture the INS and the local compact (as discussed in chapter 13).

Notes

1. Other elements contribute to explaining the everyday work of INS officers, including key historical crystallizations and organizational socialization (Heyman 1995) and caseload demands and subsequent discretionary justice (Harwood 1986). Janet Gilboy (1991, 1992) deftly connects INS officer handling of caseload pressures and other aspects of discretion to feedback from political interests in the larger society.

2. It is worth contrasting this "from the ground up" transformation of the INS with the reshuffling of immigration bureaucracies proposed by the Commission on Immigration Reform (Migration News 1997b). The Commission proposes that legal immigration processing (e.g., INS Asylum and Adjudications branches) be given to the Department of State, which already issues overseas visas. The rump INS, including Inspections, would be dedicated entirely to law enforcement. Greater authority over immigration employment issues would be given to the Department of Labor (which currently has a small but significant set of duties in setting conditions for occupational immigrant and nonimmigrant visas). The rearrangement possibly would make for a more rational clustering of responsibilities in upper management, while it possibly also would confuse the routine transfer of information about immigrants that is mostly concentrated inside the INS right now. But it misses the larger point. The visa service of the Department of State is the lowest status, most overworked, most routinized, and probably most indifferent segment of that agency. Moving immigration services from INS to State promises little modification of the underlying problems. The local-compact approach directly addresses the need for professionals exercising creativity and flexibility in real immigration processes where enforcement and service are inextricably linked.

11
Foreign Relations

We cannot view immigration only in a national context. Migrants move within global circuits of transportation, ideas, and economics (see Kearney 1986; Portes and Walton 1981; Sassen 1988). On the other hand, the most important political arena for migration policy is the nation-state, as I argued above (see chapter 5), although once a nation like the United States commits to a flexible recruitment system, there will be opportunities for transnational relationships (see chapter 7). Furthermore, sending-area development is not a facile substitute for changing domestic U.S. politics and laws; development is long-term process, and active development initially results in more, not less, emigration (see Commission for the Study of International Migration and Cooperative Economic Development 1990:xiv).[1]

These complicated, somewhat contradictory observations pose several questions for the local-compact approach. First, will the general tendency of migrants to move from developing to developed nations overwhelm the local compacts' efforts to regulate numbers via recruitment systems? Is walling off the border the only option, or given that that does not work now, is there no policy approach capable of tempering the migration consequences of global inequality? I will suggest that local compacts *can* influence migration decisions by providing more realistic information and more rational decision-making situations via immigrant recruitment networks, but I do not offer this as a Panglossian solution. The reality is that movement along established migratory paths is strong and will continue, given rapid but extremely unequal economic development inside and between nations. Second, will the local-compact approach contribute to sustainable development in the sending area? Is there any evidence now that will allow us to infer developmental effects? If the compacts contribute to sustainable development, this is a good in itself, leaving aside any role it would have in regulating migratory flows.

It is helpful to have a dynamic model of migration in world development in order to address both sets of questions. Tomas Hammar, Grete Brochmann, Kristof Tamas, and Thomas Faist give two important starting-points, that people do not just move because regions of the world are highly unequal, and that we should inquire into the causes of immobility as well as migration (see Faist 1997; Hammar and Tamas 1997). They suggest looking at migration and immobility at three levels that should be familiar to anthropologists: the macrolevel, global development and major inequalities; the mesolevel, social networks of migration linking sending and receiving areas; and the microlevel, household decisions whether to move or not. Poor people do not migrate just because national incomes are unequal; they migrate along recruitment networks. These authors see mesolevel networks as allocating "assets" (cultural and social as well as economic), some of which encourage migration (e.g., preexisting connections to jobs in the receiving location), while others encourage immobility (e.g., nontransferrable local cultural and political capital). I suggest that local compacts could shape, to a significant degree, access to promigration assets in the United States.

By shaping assets, local compacts could make international inequalities (the macrolevel) relevant versus irrelevant to migratory networks (the mesolevel) and through them, to household decisions (the microlevel); this replies to the rhetorical fear that global economic differences will overwhelm the compacts. For example, a compact that already had as many entrants as local sponsors employed and would pay for would not allocate more promigration assets in the form of approved jobs, housing, and so on. Speculative migration might continue, however, depending on how effective and meaningful was the network transmittal of information. If networks are fairly effective at getting the word home, we can expect fewer prospective immigrants to migrate. The aggregated information from U.S. compacts could shape migratory volume at a global scale. (Each compact would operate locally but they would tend to aggregate into more or less collective national migration policies.) Thus my argument is posited on some degree of network effectiveness in transmitting information about migratory assets, an assertion that can be explored through actual ethnographic observations.

What are the requirements of effective network action in this model? Networks are the migrants themselves talking, via phone and letter, to their families and communities back home. Such networks must accurately inform prospective migrants whether sponsors are available. Their messages must meaningfully affect choices of sending individuals and households. Networks must more or less accurately speak to transnational communities the decisions made by local communities inside the United States. Conversely, effective networks must voice sending-area interests in U.S. compacts through migrant-patron combinations and established immigrant associations.

"Effectiveness," then, depends on the clarity and rationality of immigrant-home communications. Sarah Mahler's (1995) ethnography of Central and South Americans on Long Island challenges that assumption. Immigrants make decisions on the basis of misleading information about U.S. life; they especially fail to weigh enticing earnings, even in poorly paid jobs, against the cost of living in the United States. Lies and deceptive truths sent home from existing migrants play major roles in misestimation. One immigrant had Mahler take pictures of him in front of new model cars that did not belong to him so that he could send the photographs home. The ethnographer argues that migrants are unwilling to admit their straitened circumstances, the crowded garage-attic apartments and frustrating periods without work, while in the land of hope. She also plausibly argues that people back home do not want to hear the complete truth about migration. Gifts sent home by emigres reinforce their exaggerated optimism. Such gifts reflect not their high purchasing power but the intense pressure to give away their small surpluses. Portrayals of U.S. consumption received in sending nations add to the illusion, at least for Mahler's urban middle and working class Latin American informants.

One particular concern is that even if potential migrants in the sending area did have accurate information about jobs, costs, and life in the United States, they might migrate anyway because of factors at home. This would make the recruitment approach less effective. In the personal migration histories from Mexico collected by Luisa Gabayet and Silvia Lailson (1987–1990), people migrated after they encountered problems (their own loss of a job, another wage-earning family member's illness) that interfered with the domestic economy in the sending nation. They used information from kin in the United States to decide where and how to go, not whether to go. In other words, basic migratory decisions did seem impervious to decisions emanating from afar. Would such decisions, as idiosyncratic as they seem, overwhelm the regulatory capacity of local compacts? Would bad times in Mexico or Korea cause an outpouring of migrants to the United States? There is reason to think so.

The viability of household economies inside a sending nation can be aggregated. In nations that have undergone rapid capitalist economic development, many people depend completely on labor and commodity markets; then when these nations suffer depressions and recessions, people leave in droves to resuscitate their household economies. If there are international networks to get out, they will follow them. This "iron-law" of capitalist migration was as true of England, Germany, and Italy of the 19th century as it is of Thailand and Turkey in the 20th century (Massey 1987–1990). When national and global development causes greater instability of household economies, such as in Mexico today (Selby et al. 1990), the signals from compacts in the United States are less likely to be effective. Speculative kin migrants expelled by personal economic events overseas might overwhelm localities. This would challenge the logistical capacity of compacts, and more dangerously, might upset the political compromises inside receiving areas of the United

States. Thus, the constructive local-compact approach to global migration would be significantly helped by a radical reform of dependent development (e.g., Franke and Chasin 1994) on a world scale, with significant redistribution of wealth to more households, rather than, as at present, taking from the many to give to the few.

Neither the logic of household response to crises nor the emotional dynamics of migration seem propitious for local compacts. If Mahler's arguments hold true across a variety of cases, then migrant communication biases decisions to increase entries to higher volumes than can be decently supported by their niche in the United States. But there is some hope that the local-compact, flexible-migration system might reduce these distortions, that is, that it might work better at regulating global flows than the crude numerical system we have now. Undocumented status, in particular, can be eliminated; importantly, it accounts for much of the behavior reported by Mahler (1995). Illegal immigrants begin their life in the United States burdened by debts for "travel agencies," smugglers, bribes, and so on. All migrants, legal or not, pay out a vast set of social funds from very low earnings at erratic jobs. They repay migration debts; they cover high expenses for rent, transportation, and sometimes childcare; on top of that, they accumulate a surplus to send or bring home. The immigrants Mahler knew suffered from enormous pressures, including failing to meet their own expectations. Under such circumstances, distorted communication, hidden suffering, and wishful bragging are hardly surprising. A more secure and less costly system for entry would remove the burdens of smuggling debt, while local-compact support for decent housing, childcare, and so on would alleviate immediate economic pressures. The clarity of immigration in a predictable, above-board regulatory system would help relieve the emotional contradictions that Mahler diagnosed.

The local-compact system also might improve the transmission of information and resources involved in sending-region development, and thus increase migration's contribution to global human development. For reasons laid out above, I define human development as an increase in the viability of household economies. The use of immigrant remittances and returnee skills in development depends most on the broad economic vitality of the sending region and community (see Arroyo et al. 1987–1990; Durand and Massey 1992; Rogers 1987–1990). Predictable and secure migration, however, does make a difference, as Catherine Colby (1997) found out in her study of Mixtec (indigenous Mexican) migrant agricultural workers. These people went either to a legal, temporary migrant-labor program in Ontario, Canada, or migrated to the United States, many without documents. In the Canadian program, migration itself was legal (eliminating the cost of smugglers), and the airfare was paid by the employer, so immigrants did not have to take out loans in advance of migration to pay for transportation. Also, the Canadian program had a mandatory paycheck deduction savings program that increased the size of remittances home compared to the United States. Departure from Canada was mandatory. Given these differences, Colby found that

> Significantly larger remittances by migrants to Canada make goals (usually material consumption) accessible in a shorter amount of time, leaving financial resources available for investment in small businesses or children's educations earlier in the households' cycles.
>
> These larger remittances also give households dependent on Canadian migration a chance to take agricultural risks through the application of new crops or technologies such as small-scale irrigation construction.
>
> Families with migrants in Canada have the emotional and financial security that the head of the household will return with significant savings, a stability not seen in families dependent on migrants to the United States.
>
> Labor migrants to Canada have the financial resources to sponsor ritual relationships and the costly community fiestas during the winter months. . . .
>
> The sending community is able to include and count on migrants to Canada to fulfill, or pay someone to fulfill, political obligations and leadership responsibilities.
>
> Migration to Canada, unlike migration to the United States and Mexico City, allows families to invest not only in their households in the sending community, but also in the home community itself. Migrants continue to focus on the sending community, not locations elsewhere, for the future and the future of their descendants. [Colby 1997:36]

Colby cautions us that migration in the U.S context is very different from the Canadian case, much larger and less tightly controlled, so that her findings can only be generalized cautiously. We can learn from this case the developmental benefits of predictable, secure, and legal immigration, not only in the economic domain but also in social and cultural qualities of life. A flexible migration system, permitting dual nationality and legal movement, conducted in a public situation providing confidence and security to migrant savers and remitters, would help such initiatives. Some positive effects that Colby discovered, however, come from the highly controlled and temporary aspects of the Canadian contract system, which differs from the definitely open-ended migratory arrangement that I propose. While the local-compact system does not broach the large questions of global human development, and while local compacts are significantly limited by these broader contexts, local compacts can discourage xenophobia and encourage the sense of humanity needed for change on a world scale.

Notes

1. Both critical and constructive perspectives abound on migration and sending-area development (for a start, see Durand and Massey 1992 and citations therein; Commission for the Study of International Migration and Cooperative Economic Development 1987-1990, vols. 1, 2, and Supplement, *passim*).

12
Unresolved Challenges and Dilemmas

The alternative immigration plan undoubtedly has many flaws. Some are flaws of incompleteness, my failure to anticipate and specify details about various requirements and contingencies. I am not particularly concerned with those flaws, but I am with the challenges that threaten to undermine the alternative as a whole. I list such challenges sincerely, the aim being to give an honest account of the cons as well as the pros of what I advocate. It is unreasonable, however, to seize upon the existence of challenges as reasons to dismiss the alternative as implausible. The status quo is necessarily plausible, since it exists (no matter how many flaws it has); inevitably, alternatives will seem less possible than what we now have.

(1) The alternative immigration system is unlikely to be enacted, given the anti-immigrationism of the last 15 years in U.S. politics. Potential exists, however, for a reversal in U.S. attitudes toward immigration, because the constellation of symbols and meanings in American public discourse about immigrants has positive as well as negative elements. Espenshade and Calhoun's (1993:209–210) poll of Californians uncovered an ideology of America as a land of opportunity, which the authors show supports favorable policies toward immigrants. (Also see Juan Perea's [1997b] analysis of "Statue of Liberty" imagery.) Immigration-restriction interpretations now dominate but the symbolic constellation could readily swing toward more liberal interpretations of opportunity. This presents a "chicken-or-egg" dilemma, since the alternative immigration policy aims to alter the symbolic constellation, yet such a shift would need to happen before it could be enacted. At least, there is potential for change; if the current U.S. path of massive escalation at the border proves to be an expensive and troublesome failure, interest in alternatives may surface.

That alternatives are unlikely seems a nearly unavoidable objection to any visionary proposal coming from anthropology; our knowledge of the range of human history and human possibility does not fit the status quo well. The political arenas of the moment should not restrict our thinking; we ought not abandon our values without a fight. Anyway, it is hard to predict which idea will thrive, and which will be condemned to dusty rest in books. Even if the alternative immigration plan is stillborn as a plan, it is a powerful exercise in criticizing the present. By counterposing detailed alternatives, the contrasts reveal subtle and taken-for-granted practices, assumptions, and governing interests of the status quo. The greatest weakness of the present U.S. immigration system is not the numbers of people who enter, or even those who are arrested. The contrast with a system of mutual personhood and moral regulation demonstrates that the greatest trouble of the present is the rising fear, especially an "abstract" fear, of immigrants, and its political consequent, the escalation of force. The alternative's greatest weakness is, perhaps, a nervousness generated because it relies for a national immigration policy on a disaggregated regulatory system, the compacts and contacts of people themselves; we cannot know how many people would enter. The alternative, however, provides hope that the present political scene does not: that trust should be the prerequisite and product of openness and flexibility, that dictation and regulation from above may diminish.

(2) The local-compact system might discourage immigration by attributing costs to sponsors (employers or existing immigrant networks, but the former especially). The proposal would open legal recruitment without numerical restriction. Costs and local petitions numbers are supposed to regulate the actual immigration volume. As an empirical matter, we cannot know in advance if petition taxes would lessen immigration; we do not know the demand elasticity for new immigrants in the vast range of affected labor markets. We do know which current employers publically demand immigrant labor. The direct petitioners and political fighters for immigrants are agribusiness, software and electronics companies, universities, hospitals, and so on. Most of the latter demand educated labor. Otherwise, U.S. employers let immigrants supply themselves, legally or illegally, thus hinting at a low degree of commitment to supporting recruitment. Importantly, the local-compact system aims not to liberalize immigration, but to reduce abstract fear of immigrants. The levied costs would be a matter for democratic decision making. They would pay for key functions in community life: schools, police, housing, and so on. Were the local compact to raise costs so high as to discourage immigration, either deliberately aiming for that end or just inadvertently, it would be the participants' due choice.

A considerable worry is that the migrants and their recruiters (employers, coethnics, etc.) would avoid compact taxes by dropping from the legal system into the black market, that is, reverting to illegal immigration. The INS would have to return to enforcement, now in the neighborhoods dense with migrants and businesses, since they would collect local-compact levies. (They would not arrest persons since a paid person is a legal person in the new system.) I cannot in all honesty dismiss this problem; any system of laws causes a counterpart possibility of a black market. Usually, enforcement by itself is not enough to halt a black market. Only the general moral climate, the mutual regulation of society, checks such a market. If the legitimacy of local compacts is profound, and if this legitimacy penetrates ethnic communities and all the diverse business sectors, few persons will enter the migrant black market even given the explicit cost advantage. In the United States today, immigration laws clearly have little moral authority among the employers of undocumented workforces; the local compacts would succeed or fail according to whether they change that.

(3) Alternatively, employers might embrace an immigration system that gave them a central role in deciding who was recruited, and thus who immigrated through the local compact—even if it cost them money. They might use immigration petitions to reward favored employees and punish restive ones. The INS, in this scenario, would become the unwitting tool of discipline for employers. For example, the local INS manager would ensure that the immigrants were legally recruited and in residence according to an employer's specific petition. (An immigrant, once entered, will be permanently legal, even if the employer does not pay her or his fees; but the employer does influence whose kin are petitioned for next.) Indeed, INS managers might become more than an "unwitting tool." They could become quite cozy with employers (a "captured bureaucracy") given the intensive contact between INS managers and local politicians, employers, and ethnic representatives, who might actually be informal labor brokers.[1] More generally, an immigration system designed to increase mutual moral regulation is inherently inclined toward social control.

The precise design of the proposal might mitigate the harshest tools of control. Immigrants would not be temporary contract laborers. Once recruited, they would have permanent residence rights in the United States. Contracts would not bind them to an employer, or even a sector. They could move about the local area and the nation looking for alternative work. (Some limitations might be imposed by the terms of exchange agreements across compacts, and by the INS use of nonmandatory referrals to move migrants from one compact to another.)

One danger is that the local-compact system might result in segregated communities in which immigrants with their employer-supported houses and neighborhoods are tolerated, but regarded badly and treated even worse. The situation described by Martha Menchaca (1995) for Mexicano agricultural laborers in Santa Paula, California, needs to be guarded against. However, we already have legally isolated and covert communities of undocumented settlers, and a virulent delocalized ideology of hostility to migrants, so it would be difficult to justify the status quo because of the risks of the alternative.

With respect to the business capture of local compacts, the alternative immigration proposal demands a radical shift in the relative power of host community versus corporation. In the status quo, business "captures" localities without the reciprocal local capture of business. For example, high plains meatpackers make enormous demands on the host communities, for example for investments in water supply. Such negotiations almost entirely assume that benefits flow toward the corporation, because the community is anxious to get a major investor. Yet the terms of bargaining could be partly reversed, if communities made better use of their resources. As Stull, Broadway, and Griffith point out:

> Communities are far from powerless in dealing with major food processors; indeed, industries locate in particular locales because of their special resources, such as water and livestock. These resources allow communities to bargain on favorable terms with potential employers. [1995:6]

In related fashion, Cynthia Ninivaggi (1994) provides a devastating portrait of the self-aggrandizing and nondemocratic role of a business association in a Philadelphia enterprise zone. The business association was the recipient of socially redistributed resources, and its mode of operation was to maximize receipt of public subsidies. How would the compact differ from the enterprise zone? The basic idea behind the enterprise zone is that taxes are reduced, and resources flow toward businesses, whereas the concept in the local compact is that taxes are imposed, and resources flow from the immigrant sponsor (e.g., employer) toward the larger collective good, the community and the settling immigrants. Given this premise, I suggest that the compact would not be manipulated purely for elite benefits, but would be an arena of negotiation in which resources and reciprocities can go in several directions.

(4) The alternative immigration plan might worsen the condition of Latinos and blacks if compacts admit many low-skilled immigrants who compete with U.S. minorities for jobs. It might lower wage rates and reduce their total share of employment. This would not be an inherent feature of the alternative immigration plan, since it would not be a migration-increasing plan per se, but a change in the locus of participation. Nevertheless, we ought to have serious concern about harming U.S. blacks and Latinos. They have a strong justice claim on the United States since racial inequality has been officially and tacitly promulgated for so

long. We also respect the prudential argument that it is destructive to constrain career opportunities for young blacks and Latinos. Thus we are compelled to question rigorously the alternative immigration plan.

A compilation of studies by Urban Institute researchers (Fix and Passel 1994:49–51) shows the following impacts of new immigration on labor markets. Low-skill immigrants somewhat depress the labor market position of all low-skilled workers, though foreign competition adds significantly more to this effect; as a result, immigration increases wage inequality in the United States in a small but measurable way. Immigration has no negative impacts for black workers as a whole, but the effects differ by location. Places with high immigration but also a prospering local economy do not show negative effects on blacks of job competition; such competition may occur (and be well known to local people) but the high level of employment transcends its effects. Places with weak regional labor markets, however, do transmit to blacks harmful effects of immigration (even at lower-than-national average rates of influx). Among blacks, those with lower skills suffer the most competition, in part because employers rely on immigrant recruitment networks, which are simple and inexpensive, thus excluding nonimmigrants. Let us note in passing that one aim of the local-compact system is to acknowledge and use these powerful recruiting networks, but to charge them social costs, potentially altering the calculations of employers. Most dramatically, the compiled studies show that new immigrants do the greatest labor market harm to older, settled immigrants. For that reason, immigration particularly hurts U.S. Latinos.

The labor market studies are ambiguous but do not manifest large harms. Such studies, however,in the classic "all things being equal" fashion of economics, accept the historical context of U.S. society: black and Latino bargaining power is depressed, and they generally do not coalesce into strong mass labor organizations. The labor economist Vernon Briggs (1992) presents a strong argument that all things are *not* equal because of immigration after 1965. Extensive immigration depressed the organizational power of low-skilled laborers, undercutting the United Farm Workers and other minority unionization efforts. Advances for U.S. minorities, for example, the Civil Rights laws, occurred in the 1960s through the early 1970s, but were subdued and even rolled back since the escalation of immigration from the 1970s to the present.

Briggs is a strong advocate of immigration restriction. More importantly, he directs attention to the societal bargaining power of U.S. minorities, their strengths and weaknesses in institutional struggles that generate surface market conditions. Increasing the bargaining power of U.S. minorities ought to be a crux of any positive strategy for justice in the United States. Conversely, the damaging effect of immigration on bargaining power ought to be taken seriously. The local-compact's role in altering bargaining power is unclear. Compacts would favor loosely regulated and almost automatically legal immigration, so they might increase migration substantially. (Although we cannot know if they would increase total migration or simply legalize undocumented immigration.) They would assess significant social taxes on migration sponsors (especially employers), thus shifting the economic calculations toward domestic workers over immigrants. In the allocation of the compact revenues, some portion would go to bureaucracies that served all local residents, migrant and host alike, such as police and schools; other revenues, however, would be specifically directed to immigrants (such as new house construction). This allocation could be unjust, and thus resented, in a society, like the United States, where little such support goes to the domestic poor. The local-compact negotiation, above all, could be the locus for either improving or worsening domestic minority bargaining power. Properly participatory, compact negotiations would offer an arena for U.S. minorities to bargain for significant concessions from local employers, politicians, and other powers-that-be, in exchange for acquiescence in migration recruitment. Local-compact negotiations, however, are subject to "capture" like any other process. They could become a closed circle of employers, politicians, service providers, and immigrant brokers, with little but superficial minority participation.

The concerns raised here form a classic moral dilemma, the clash of two compelling claims responding to substantial harms: the present immigration system, with its harm of a covert, undocumented population, and the justice claims that are nowhere being fulfilled for U.S. blacks and Latinos.[2] The only answer is to be conscious of both claims, and thus shape our actions for both domains at once, a burden that given the wealth of this nation is not beyond our capabilities. Thus a morally adequate implementation of the alternative immigration plan would require deliberate acts to increase the bargaining power of low-skilled domestic workers, especially minorities. It would require laws that will strengthen unionization. It would require a reversal of the trend toward the undermining of civil rights laws. It would require greater attention to urban planning, with serious restrictions on the mobility of real estate and manufacturing capital in order to halt the destruction of cities. Within that urban context, and also many farm labor locales, it would require a massive investment in public education instead of a flight from public schools.

It would be easy enough to deploy these observations to dismiss the immigration alternative. A reply rests, I think, in the real political agendas of anti-immigration proponents who use social justice for domestic minorities in their rhetoric. Briggs comes to immigration-restrictionism, I suspect, as a liberal Democrat of the Kennedy-Johnson persuasion. He genuinely fuses the advocacy of lowering migration levels with increased bargaining power for poor Americans. That is a combination rarely found in anti-immigrant politics, however. As Governor Wilson and others in California demonstrate, the anti-immigrant movement overlaps the assaults on affirmative action, and indeed on virtually everything listed above. If anti-immigrationism outside the black community came with a sincere concern for U.S. minorities, it might be a more persuasive resolution to the moral dilemma described here. It is not, however, and I thus hold that a conscientious application of the local participatory system offers better hope for moral action in this challenging terrain.

(5) Some critics (e.g., Bouvier and Grant 1994) argue that immigration to the United States should be drastically reduced, if not eliminated, because it is detrimental to the sustainability of the human adaptation to the global environment. The argument pivots from migration to total U.S. population, then to national consumption, and finally global impact. The reader should understand that the alternative immigration plan calls for localities to set numerical levels; thus it would not inherently expand or shrink the total immigration volume, depending instead on the aggregation of local decisions. Since the proposal is generally critical of immigration restrictionism and strong policing controls, it is reasonable to posit a conflict with *this* "environmentalist" stance.

We must distinguish between two different issues. Environmental impacts in the United States come from the high consumption levels of all U.S. residents, and of the U.S. production system as a whole (Postel 1994). They do not happen simply because there are more people. More people, from migration and fertility, do lead to greater impacts, but only indirectly, for the proximate cause is the pattern of consumption and waste outputs. Therefore, environmental impact is principally an issue of the nation as a whole, and not specifically of immigration. On the other hand, demographic scenarios, whether aggressive or cautious, pro- or anti-immigrant, all show that new migrants will add to U.S. population growth in the next century (e.g., Bouvier and Grant 1994; Passel and Fix 1994:39–40).[3] This happens mostly not by the addition of immigrants, but by their subsequent fertility. If there are more Americans, *and* a variety of factors add up to Americans consuming too much energy and putting out waste, then immigration worsens the U.S.'s environmental impact. But immigration's effect is mediated through processes such as the U.S. automotive transportation system and metropolitan sprawl, residential and commercial heating and lighting, demand for paper and construction wood, and so on—all of which merit attention in and of themselves, as well as through the proxy of migrants.

Leon Bouvier and Lindsey Grant's book (1994) has an undertone of protecting present U.S. standards of consumption, though it is internally inconsistent in this regard. For example, the authors counterpose, at the very beginning, a vastly overpopulated society having a low standard of living versus,

> At the other extreme, one may imagine a society built on the much maligned automobile, where every potential driver has a car to suit his or her taste and yet the environment is not threatened. The only requirement in that scenario is that there can be very few cars, and therefore very few people. [1994:4]

This angle may be found in several other places in the book (e.g., 1994:54, 57, 95). In a moral framework of mutual exchange, we cannot accept the idea of penalizing immigrants by arresting them in order to preserve an environmentally harmful consumption pattern for the few. We ought to consider reducing U.S. population seriously, but only *in exchange for* considering reducing U.S. consumption seriously. Immigration looks very different once we link it to overconsumption.

U.S. overconsumption is deeply implicated in the entry of migrants. Immigrants labor in the making of metropolitan sprawl and in its strip-development businesses. Food is provided to American tables at all seasons, in vast quantities, over great distances, and at remarkable cost to the environment, via pesticide and energy use. Juan-Vicente Palerm links the rapid growth of immigrant Latino farmworker communities in California "to the transformation of the state's agricultural industry, which now thrives on the production of high-value, premium specialty fruit and vegetable crops to supply a seemingly insatiable demand by consumers, living mostly in rich industrialized nations, who are willing to pay premium prices for fancy produce" (1995:2). As Oaxacans come to California to labor, and baby carrots are shipped to New York for sale, the scale of consumption is delocalized.

What can the local-compact, flexible-migration plan do about delocalization of scale? Quite a bit, I hold. Immigration politics is already, in considerable part, an indirect debate over growth, sprawl, and scale, as in Monterey Park, California (Horton 1995). In that suburb of Los Angeles, uncontrolled real estate development by both Anglo and Chinese Americans led to a slow-growth political movement with complex host and immigrant (often second-generation) components. The compact offers a way to negotiate local and regional size. By assessing social costs to immigrant recruiters, the compact would temper the economic advantages of delocalization and sprawl. More importantly, the compact offers the possibility of Americans taking responsibility for, and participating in, scale as a vital issue.

In a very important work, Herman Daly and John Cobb (1994) show that economists ignore, and yet a democratic people cannot afford to neglect, the size of the physical economy (the economy not just measured in dollars but in physical inputs, outputs, and natural capital). They also show that scale is important for the environmental sustainability of the nation and the world. Daly and Cobb strongly favor the restriction of immigration, especially national efforts to halt undocumented immigration. Their immigration position is, however, a secondary feature of an overriding concern with democratic choice about scale. The local-compact system would offer a meaningful opportunity for people to decide on key components of "scale," such as numbers of new residents, impacts of capital investment, and housing. Importantly, it would allow the development of greater consciousness about scale as something that a democratic people can and should determine. Attention to broad aspects of scale, such as optimal population size, capital accumulation and mobility, and the character of consumption, might then come forward. A wave of democratic choices across society might reverse the tendencies toward delocalization and sprawl, both fine-tuning migration to locales and indirectly reducing the consumption-driven demand for migrants. Environmentally oriented migration restriction might triumph, but if so, it would respond to decisions to reduce overconsumption and overgrowth in communities and the nation as a whole, rather than from blame and hatred directed at abstract "immigrants." Rappaport challenged us to think about the combination of humane and ecological values. A good start is to explore direct democratic participation on questions of scale.[4]

(6) The flaws of the immigration proposal are manifest. But what are the options? We (the people of the United States) can stick with the current path, increasing migration law enforcement at the border. We do not know whether that will reduce undocumented immigration in the future; it also leaves open the question whether it is desirable to decrease immigration at all. We *do* know that the build-up at the border has not worked in the last 15 years. We could respond to its failure by setting up a national identification card or national electronic identity registry. Such a registry would have to identify every person in the United States, including citizens. (Otherwise undocumented aliens would claim to be citizens not required to bear identification.) A national identity would make possible the internal control of migration, principally by making the laws against employment of unauthorized aliens effective. It would thus require extensive internal policing. Any sort of numerical control

system would require this kind of enforcement if it were to keep migration in the legal category and out of the undocumented category. This would be true whether we chose high or low numbers of legal immigrants, because the protean nature of migration will bring some persons to enter outside of numerical restrictions. Thus, if we chose to stick with the present path of immigration control, we will either end with ineffective results or with an effective police system based on national-identity control.[5]

We might also choose to decrease the criticism of immigrants, reverse the denial of social distributions, and halt the escalation of the INS at the border. We might put up with the present ineffectual system of employer sanctions, rather than putting teeth into them. We might also seek greater due process and fairness in asylum adjudications. This "liberalization" alternative might increase the current legal immigration ceiling, or it might judge the current U.S. rate of legal admissions high by international standards and therefore acceptable. This is the tacit policy of defenders of the existing immigrants against the rising tide of xenophobia. But what do defenders argue for? To accept the present immigration system in general—the division between legal and illegal immigrants? The continuing smuggling and danger at the border, or the covert life inside the United States? Even if we increased legal admissions, it is likely that present migration chains would send further illegal immigrants to the United States. Would we have the INS use an identity card then? The fundamental problem is that a defense of immigrants in particulars is not a constructive vision of immigration, and tacitly endorses the status quo with its problems.

Or we could make most, if not all immigrants, into "persons" in the sense of being recognized as legal residents of the nation. This could not, however, simply consist of opening up admissions, since present migration chains can readily launch speculative migrants to the United States. The nation is not prepared in terms of housing, schools, and so on. A proposal for legalization of all immigration must establish some form of regulation internal to those migration chains. We are thus drawn to the local-compact, flexible-recruitment system outlined here. As I said, its flaws are manifest—but so are the flaws of the alternatives.

Notes

1. Analogously, agribusiness "captured" the INS during the Bracero contract labor period, because of their shared involvement in administering immigrant control (Calavita 1992; Galarza 1964, 1977).

2. In an article very helpful for clarifying thought, Judith Lichtenberg (1983) reviews immigrant and domestic economic needs as clashing moral imperatives.

3. Migration's effects on global population are less obvious. Whereas in-migration leads to a rise in any given nation's population, on a world scale it is only

a transfer of population, not an increase in numbers. International migration may affect global fertility, but its effects are ambiguous and we still know little. Recent immigrant women in the United States, especially Latin Americans, have lower fertility than they would have had in their origin country, though higher than native-born U.S. women (Jasso and Rosenzweig 1990:382–396). The fertility rate of the U.S.-born daughters of Mexican immigrant women is lower yet, though it remains higher than Anglo Americans (Bean et al. 1984). Thus, while immigration to the United States causes an increase in U.S. population (both directly and via fertility), it causes a decrease in net global fertility *of the migrants*. On the other hand, emigration might subsidize high fertility and survival rates in sending/remittance receiving areas. Virginia Abernethy (1993:41) suggests that families decide to have many children because they expect some children to emigrate. Abernethy's citations are tenuous: she cites one modest case from modern-day St. Vincent and the Grenadines (Brittain 1990), and a 19th-century study from the United Kingdom (Friedlander 1983, both cited in Abernethy 1993:41). Abernethy (1993) strenuously attempts to make a global population case for U.S. immigration restriction. Her book is undoubtedly correct in its broadest point, that we cannot count on an automatic, asocial "demographic transition" to bring global fertility down. Beyond that, however, her models of fertility are naive. She views the third world household as a simple responder—more resources, more children—while ignoring the complex interactions of particular types of resources and household decisions—children's education, children's labor, varied rural and urban household economies, women's power, and so on. Such household dynamics are now significantly reducing fertility in major migrant sending nations, such as Mexico (Alba 1989). Furthermore, the role of international migration in such dynamics is unknown. It is likely that total world population affects the volume of migration, but the question at stake in the environment-migration debate is the inverse: how does immigration affect global overpopulation? This we simply do not know.

4. A perspicacious reviewer of this monograph noticed the potential contradiction between my critique of delocalization and my advocacy of a recruitment-based migration system that might dislocate people. My reply is that, in the midst of an existing, massive global migration system, I have tried to envision a scheme that relocalizes responsibility and commitment (e.g., of employers and politicians), and in some cases promotes paired relationships that emphasize grounded responsibility in both locales, even though they are physically separated (e.g., for transnational migrants). Given the undoubted persistence of global movement, this is probably the best strategy of "extrication" (Coady 1991; see ch. 3, n. 2) available to us.

5. One school of thought holds that it is necessary to restrict immigration, especially of illegal immigration, and even to lower the numbers of new, legal Americans, so as to calm the ruffled feathers of U.S. politics. Only then do these authors feel we can find support for more pro-immigrant social services and legal rights (Espenshade and Calhoun 1993). Others hold a similar position that stronger law enforcement and similar measures that address the gap between policy and reality can reduce anti-immigrationism (Cornelius et al. 1994). In either case, this rationalizes supporting the goals and concrete policies of strong anti-immigrationists, since that will calm them down (or undermine their support). This defeatist stance accepts the existing anti-immigration, mass national politics arena; it does not contemplate changing that arena itself.

13
Concluding Observations

Present anthropology places its hope for constructive action in the hands of immediate populations, in their meetings, leaders, and movements from below. Perhaps this emphasis fits the experiences and wishes of individual ethnographers, engaged with particular people. The constructive engaged anthropology offered here differs—it is a plan offered, top-down, by one academic writer. But it complements the other approach. If localism has a weakness, it is providing little vision of what political frameworks make possible for on-the-ground participation, and how these various local engagements merge, from bottom-up, into social change. The plan here is, with all its inadequacies, aimed at increasing the sphere of possible participation, the domain of mutual and beneficial regulation of immigration between networked migrant and located host. If the personal experience of the ethnographer draws hope from the local, the worldview of anthropology—our grand worldview—draws hope from large questions: what have been and what can be human conditions? We cannot take the role of dictating, as all-knowing scholars, to participants, but we abandon part of our talents, part of what we offer, if we do not bring forth an anthropological vision in bracing facts and novel ideas.

One danger of a visionary exercise is that it potentially rationalizes dictating to people. Utopias, being both systematic and appealing, motivate the imposition of "good systems" on people. No framework of ideas, however, is more valuable than the people that it supposedly benefits. The perils of utopia are an unavoidable criticism of my exhortations. I do not think that this negates the general advice to anthropologists to do constructive writing. To resolve this, we must be very clear about the status of our writing: it is advice to people in general; they will take it or leave it as they choose. They should not be made to take it because it is "correct." We do state our positions because of a faith in our disciplinary knowledge. We think we are "more right," at any given time, than those writers with alternative perspectives (e.g., economics). To deny this is to be naive about why we write what we write and teach what we teach (see Bowlin and Stromberg 1997). But contingent "right" does not mean we have more "rights" than others to decide what would be best to do.[1] "Best to do" is a personal choice, affected by listening to, but a level of freedom higher than, our momentary "best knowledge" (see Midgely 1994:103–106). Understood in this way, we can justify making some constructive and systematic statements, without claiming the right to infallible action from a utopia.

The exercise of confronting an ideal vision with the tangles of historical, processual social science has proven productive. For example, the admirable work of many scholars on specific recruitment and network chains shatters the conventional immigration policy debates that concern crude numbers of admissions under simplistic social categories. An immigration ideal has to encompass recruitment chains. Just as the immigration plan benefits from political economy and other processual social sciences, so it contributes to them. Radical, historical political economy seems to be a dismal science indeed, for it locates systems of inequality, segmentation, and power in the past, leaving little room for concern with the present. It also gives us so many instances of people fractured into oppositions that we are left with no sense of how we combine to fulfill decently our human requisites. Those troubles can be rectified, not by ignoring the past or painting rosy pictures, but by considering how human capacities, differently directed, might construct our daily lives differently.

The immigration example, by revealing its own limitations, shows a compelling need for anthropology to explore the intersection between purely human and human-natural values, as Rappaport (1995) insisted. A human value in immigration, shared mutual personhood, is not necessarily a value in a human-adaptationist view of the global environment. There, perhaps, the conscious mastery of scale is more compelling. We could promote anthropology if we would boast a little more about how well-suited we are to study humans and nature together, but it is perhaps more to the point to exhort ourselves to set forth affirmative visions of human use of, adaptation to, and respect for the environment. In parallel with my comments on political economy, we should seek a positive as well as a critical political ecology (see Anderson 1996 on the former; see Greenberg and Park 1994; Sheridan 1995 on the latter).

Anthropology today must change. We have looked inward, struggling with our flawed ways of knowing and our legacy as a discipline that comes from only one region of humanity and yet claims to study all humanity. As a result, we seem paralyzed by scholastic concerns. We devote our greatest energies to debates over epistemology—the obvious obsession of the scholar. Even the D'Andrade/Scheper-Hughes debate subtly mutated from whether and how anthropologists ought to act on the political world to how politics shapes our epistemology. Now, we need to depart our "selves." Our characteristic debate should shift from how we know things and write them down, to what we share and advocate based on what we do know, albeit imperfectly. We know about the vast increase in the scale of human occupation of the planet over time, and we know that we do not govern ourselves at the scale that we affect the earth. But we have hardly debated, let alone disagreed vituperatively, about what to do about it. The lack of conversation is disturbing. The immigration alternative proposed here is a small effort to move anthropology from the debates of the 1980s and 1990s to the debates of the 2000s.

Notes

1. I acknowledge here that some knowledge is privileged, in both authority and whose voice is likely to be disseminated: often academic or journalistic, and from the core regions and groups of the world system, but rarely anthropological, usually being derived from economics and politics. It is thus weakly the case that anthropologists' knowledge claims impinge on other people's rights to choose actions. Short of not saying anything at all, we do exert authority whenever we say things. Given this original sin, we are best off maximizing the conscious barrier I propose in the text between our faith in our knowledge and our faith in others' rights to do as they wish.

References Cited

Abernethy, Virginia
1993 Population Politics: The Choices that Shape Our Future. New York: Plenum Press.

Acuña, Rodolfo F.
1984 A Community under Siege: A Chronicle of Chicanos East of the Los Angeles River 1945–1975. Monograph No. 11. Los Angeles: Chicano Studies Research Center, University of California.

Alba, Francisco
1989 The Mexican Demographic Situation. *In* Mexican and Central American Population and U.S. Immigration Policy. Frank D. Bean, Jurgen Schmandt, and Sidney Weintraub, eds. Pp. 5–32. Austin: Center for Mexican American Studies, University of Texas.

Aleinikoff, T. Alexander
1997 The Tightening Circle of Membership. *In* Immigrants Out! The New Nativism and the Anti-Immigrant Impulse in the United States. Juan F. Perea, ed. Pp. 324–332. New York: New York University Press.

Alvarez, Robert R., Jr.
1995 The Mexican-US Border: The Making of an Anthropology of Borderlands. Annual Review of Anthropology 24:447–470.

American Friends Service Committee
1990 Human Rights at the Mexico-U.S. Border. Second Annual Report, Immigration Law Enforcement Monitoring Project. Philadelphia: American Friends Service Committee.
1992 Sealing Our Borders: The Human Toll. Third Annual Report, Immigration Law Enforcement Monitoring Project. Philadelphia: American Friends Service Committee.

Americas Watch
1992 Brutality Unchecked: Human Rights Abuses along the U.S. Border with Mexico. New York: Human Rights Watch.
1993 Frontier Injustice: Human Rights Abuses along the U.S. Border with Mexico Persist amid Climate of Impunity. New York: Human Rights Watch.
1995 Crossing the Line: Human Rights Abuses along the U.S. Border with Mexico Persist amid Climate of Impunity. New York: Human Rights Watch.

Anderson, E. N.
1996 Ecologies of the Heart: Emotion, Belief, and the Environment. Oxford: Oxford University Press.

Arroyo Alejandre, Jesús, Adrián De León Arias, and Basilia Valenzuela Varela
1987–1990 Patterns of Migration and Regional Development in the State of Jalisco, Mexico. *In* Unauthorized Migration: Addressing the Root Causes: Research Addendum, Supplement. Commission for the Study of International Migration and Cooperative Economic Development. Pp. 1–44. Washington, DC: U.S. Government Printing Office.

Bach, Robert L.
1978 Mexican Immigration and the American State. International Migration Review 12:536–558.

1993 Changing Relations: Newcomers and Established Residents in U.S. Communities. New York: Ford Foundation.

Bailey, F. G.

1996 The Civility of Indifference: On Domesticating Ethnicity. Ithaca, NY: Cornell University Press.

Bailey, Stanley, Karl Eshbach, Jacqueline Hagan, and Nestor Rodriguez

1996 Migrant Deaths at the Texas-Mexico Border, 1985–1994. Working Paper Series 96-1. Houston, TX: Center for Immigration Research, University of Houston.

Barbalet, J. M.

1988 Citizenship. Minneapolis: University of Minnesota Press.

Barry, Tom, Harry Browne, and Beth Sims

1994 Crossing the Line: Immigrants, Economic Integration, and Drug Enforcement on the U.S.-Mexico Border. The U.S.-Mexico Series, No. 3. Albuquerque, NM: The Resource Center Press.

Basch, Linda, James Peacock, Lucie Wood Saunders, and Jagna Wojcicka Sharff

N.d. Transforming Academe: In Search of a Proactive Anthropology. Washington, DC: American Ethnological Society.

Bean, Frank D., Ruth M. Cullen, Elizabeth H. Stephen, and C. Gray Swicegood

1984 Generational Differences in Fertility among Mexican Americans: Implications for Assessing Immigration Effects. Social Science Quarterly 65:573–582.

Bean, Frank D., Roland Chanove, Robert G. Cushing, Rodolfo de la Garza, Gary P. Freeman, Charles W. Haynes, and David Spener

1994 Illegal Mexican Migration and the United States/Mexico Border: The Effect of Operation Hold the Line on El Paso/Juarez. Austin, TX: Population Research Center, University of Texas at Austin.

Benjamin, Daniel K., and Roger Leroy Miller

1991 Undoing Drugs: Beyond Legalization, How We, the People, Can Retake America from the Drug Dealers, Drug Addicts, and Drug-Enforcement Agents. New York: Basic Books.

Benson, Janet E.

1994 The Effects of Packinghouse Work on Southeast Asian Refugee Families. *In* Newcomers in the Workplace: Immigrants and the Restructuring of the U.S. Economy. Louise Lamphere, Alex Stepick, and Guillermo Grenier, eds. Pp. 99–126. Philadelphia: Temple University Press.

Bertram, Eva, Morris Blachman, Kenneth Sharpe, and Peter Andreas

1996 Drug War Politics: The Price of Denial. Berkeley and Los Angeles: University of California Press.

Best, Joel

1995 Typification and Social Problems Construction. *In* Images of Issues: Typifying Contemporary Social Problems. Joel Best, ed. Pp. 1–15. New York: Walter de Gruyter.

Blumberg, Paul

1980 Inequality in an Age of Decline. New York: Oxford University Press.

Borjas, George

1990 Friends or Strangers: The Impact of Immigrants on the U.S. Economy. New York: Basic Books.

Bosniak, Linda
1997 "Nativism" the Concept: Some Reflections. *In* Immigrants Out! The New Nativism and the Anti-Immigrant Impulse in the United States. Juan F. Perea, ed. Pp. 279–299. New York: New York University Press.
Bourgois, Philippe
1995a From Jíbaro to Crack Dealer: Confronting the Restructuring of Capitalism in El Barrio. *In* Articulating Hidden Histories: Exploring the Influence of Eric R. Wolf. Jane Schneider and Rayna Rapp, eds. Pp. 125–141. Berkeley and Los Angeles: University of California Press.
1995b In Search of Respect: Selling Crack in El Barrio. Cambridge: Cambridge University Press.
Bouvier, Leon F., and Lindsey Grant
1994 How Many Americans? Population, Immigration, and the Environment. San Francisco: Sierra Club Books.
Bowlin, John R., and Peter G. Stromberg
1997 Representation and Reality in the Study of Culture. American Anthropologist 99:123–134.
Briggs, Vernon M., Jr.
1992 Mass Immigration and the National Interest. Armonk, NY: M.E. Sharpe.
Brimelow, Peter
1995 Alien Nation: Common Sense about America's Immigration Disaster. New York: Random House.
Brinkley, Joel
1994 At Immigration, Disarray and Defeat. New York Times, September 11:1.
Brittain, A. W.
1990 Migration and the Demographic Transition: A West Indian Example. Social and Economic Studies 39(3):39–64.
Broadway, Michael
1994 Beef Stew: Cattle, Immigrants, and Established Residents in a Kansas Beefpacking Town. *In* Newcomers in the Workplace: Immigrants and the Restructuring of the U.S. Economy. Louise Lamphere, Alex Stepick, and Guillermo Grenier, eds. Pp. 25–43. Philadelphia: Temple University Press.
Brown, Donald E.
1991 Human Universals. New York: McGraw-Hill.
Calavita, Kitty
1982 California's "Employer Sanctions": The Case of the Disappearing Law. Research Report Series No. 39. La Jolla, CA: Center for U.S.-Mexican Studies, University of California, San Diego.
1984 U.S. Immigration Law and the Control of Labor: 1820–1924. London: Academic Press.
1990 Employer Sanctions Violations: Toward a Dialectical Model of White-Collar Crime. Law and Society Review 24:1041–1069.
1992 Inside the State: The Bracero Program, Immigration, and the I.N.S. New York: Routledge.
Cardoso, Lawrence A.
1980 Mexican Emigration to the United States, 1897–1931. Tucson: University of Arizona Press.
Carlson, Robert G.
1996 The Political Economy of AIDS among Drug Users in the United States: Beyond Blaming the Victim or Powerful Others. American Anthropologist 98:266–278.

Carrier, James G., and Josiah McC. Heyman
1997 Consumption and Political Economy. Journal of the Royal Anthropological Institute (N.S.) 3:355–373.
Chavez, Leo R.
1988 Settlers and Sojourners: The Case of Mexicans in the United States. Human Organization 47:95–108.
1992 Shadowed Lives: Undocumented Immigrants in American Society. FT Worth, TX: Harcourt, Brace, Jovanovich College Publishers.
1997 The Construction of an Anti-Mexican Discourse: An Analysis of Popular Magazine Images. A paper presented at the 96th Annual Meeting of the American Anthropological Association, Washington, DC, November.
Chavez, Leo R., Estevan T. Flores, and Marta Lopez-Garza
1990 Here Today, Gone Tomorrow? Undocumented Settlers and Immigration Reform. Human Organization 49:193–205.
Coady, C. A. J.
1991 Politics and the Problem of Dirty Hands. *In* A Companion to Ethics. Peter Singer, ed. Pp. 373–383. Oxford, UK: Blackwell.
Cohen, Stanley
1980 Folk Devils and Moral Panics: The Creation of the Mods and Rockers. Rev. edition. New York: St. Martin's Press.
1985 Visions of Social Control: Crime, Punishment and Classification. Cambridge, England: Polity Press.
Colby, Catherine
1997 From Oaxaca to Ontario: Mexican Contract Labor in Canada and the Impact at Home. Davis, CA: California Institute of Rural Studies.
Commission for the Study of International Migration and Cooperative Economic Development
1987–1990 Unauthorized Migration: Addressing the Root Causes: Research Addendum, vol. 1, vol. 2, and Supplement. Washington, DC: U.S. Government Printing Office.
1990 Unauthorized Migration: An Economic Development Response. Washington, DC: Government Printing Office.
Conover, Ted
1987 Coyotes: A Journey through the Secret World of America's Illegal Aliens. New York: Vintage.
Cornelius, Wayne A.
1982 America in the Era of Limits: Migrants, Nativists, and the Future of U.S.-Mexican Relations. Working Papers in U.S.-Mexican Studies No. 3. La Jolla, CA: Program in United States-Mexican Studies, University of California, San Diego.
1987–1990 Labor Migration to the United States: Development, Outcomes, and Alternatives in Mexican Sending Communities. *In* Unauthorized Migration: Addressing the Root Causes: Research Addendum, vol. 1. Commission for the Study of International Migration and Cooperative Economic Development. Pp. 81–124. Washington, DC: U.S. Government Printing Office.
1989a Mexican Migration to the United States: Introduction. *In* Mexican Migration to the United States: Origins, Consequences, and Policy Options. Wayne A. Cornelius and Jorge A. Bustamante, eds. Pp. 1–21. Dimensions of U.S.-Mexican Relations, vol. 3. La Jolla, CA: Center for U.S.-Mexico Studies, University of California, San Diego.

1989b The U.S. Demand for Mexican Labor. *In* Mexican Migration to the United States: Origins, Consequences, and Policy Options. Wayne A. Cornelius and Jorge A. Bustamante, eds. Pp. 25–47. Dimensions of U.S.-Mexican Relations, vol. 3. La Jolla, CA: Center for U.S.-Mexico Studies, University of California, San Diego.

Cornelius, Wayne A., Philip L. Martin, and James F. Hollifield
1994 Introduction: The Ambivalent Quest for Immigration Control. *In* Controlling Immigration: A Global Perspective. Wayne A. Cornelius, Philip L. Martin, and James F. Hollifield, eds. Pp. 3–42. Stanford, CA: Stanford University Press.

Daly, Herman E., and John B. Cobb, Jr.
1994 For the Common Good: Redirecting the Economy toward Community, the Environment, and a Sustainable Future. 2nd edition. Boston: Beacon Press.

D'Andrade, Roy
1995 Moral Models in Anthropology. Current Anthropology 36:399–408, 420–440.

Delgado, Richard
1997 Citizenship. *In* Immigrants Out! The New Nativism and the Anti-Immigrant Impulse in the United States. Juan F. Perea, ed. Pp. 318–323. New York: New York University Press.

Dillon, Sam
1996 Agua Prieta Journal: Border Patrol vs. "Illegals": And Now, Desert Warfare. New York Times, March 26:1.

Douglas, Mary
1966 Purity and Danger: An Analysis of the Concepts of Purity and Taboo. London: Routledge and Kegan Paul.

Dumont, Louis
1977 From Mandeville to Marx: The Genesis and Triumph of Economic Ideology. Chicago: University of Chicago Press.
1986 Essays on Individualism: Modern Ideology in Anthropological Perspective. Chicago: University of Chicago Press.

Dunn, Timothy
1996 The Militarization of the U.S.-Mexico Border 1978–1992: Low-Intensity Doctrine Conflict Comes Home. Austin, TX: Center for Mexican American Studies, University of Texas at Austin.

Durand, Jorge, and Douglas S. Massey
1992 Mexican Migration to the United States: A Critical Review. Latin American Research Review 27(2):3–42.

Edmonston, Barry, and Jeffrey S. Passel, eds.
1994 Immigration and Ethnicity: The Integration of America's Newest Arrivals. Washington, DC: The Urban Institute Press.

Erickson, Ken C.
1994 Guys in White Hats: Short-Term Participant Observation among Beef-Processing Workers and Managers. *In* Newcomers in the Workplace: Immigrants and the Restructuring of the U.S. Economy. Louise Lamphere, Alex Stepick, and Guillermo Grenier, eds. Pp. 78–98. Philadelphia: Temple University Press.

Espenshade, Thomas J., and Charles A. Calhoun
1993 An Analysis of Public Opinion toward Undocumented Immigration. Population Research and Policy Review 12:189–224.

Faist, Thomas
1997 From Common Questions to Common Concepts. *In* International Migration, Immobility, and Development: Multidisciplinary Perspectives. Tomas Hammar, Grete Brochmann, Kristof Tamas, and Thomas Faist, eds. Pp. 247–276. Oxford, England: Berg.
Finkielkraut, Alain
1995 The Defeat of the Mind. Judith Friedlander, trans. New York: Columbia University Press.
Finnegan, William
1996 The New Americans. The New Yorker, March 25:6:52–71.
Fix, Michael, and Jeffrey S. Passel
1994 Immigration and Immigrants: Setting the Record Straight. Washington, DC: The Urban Institute.
Foley, Douglas E.
1990 Learning Capitalist Culture: Deep in the Heart of Tejas. Austin: University of Texas Press.
Fox, Richard G.
1995 Cultural Dis-Integration and the Invention of New Peace-Fares. *In* Articulating Hidden Histories: Exploring the Influence of Eric R. Wolf. Jane Schneider and Rayna Rapp, eds. Pp. 275–287. Berkeley and Los Angeles: University of California Press.
Fox, Robin
1989 The Search for Society: Quest for a Biosocial Science and Morality. New Brunswick, NJ: Rutgers University Press.
Franke, Richard W., and Barbara H. Chasin
1994 Kerala: Radical Reform as Development in an Indian State. 2nd edition. Oakland, CA: Institute for Food and Development Policy.
Frazer, Elizabeth, Jennifer Hornsby, and Sabina Lovibond, eds.
1992 Ethics: A Feminist Reader. Oxford, England: Blackwell.
Friedlander, D.
1983 Demographic Responses and Socioeconomic Structure: Population Processes in England and Wales in the Nineteenth Century. Demography 20:249–272.
Gabayet, Luisa, and Silvia Lailson
1987–1990 The Role of Female Wage Earners in Male Migration in Guadalajara. *In* Unauthorized Migration: Addressing the Root Causes: Research Addendum, Supplement. Commission for the Study of International Migration and Cooperative Economic Development. Pp. 75–104. Washington, DC: U.S. Government Printing Office.
Galarza, Ernesto
1964 Merchants of Labor: The Mexican Bracero Story. Santa Barbara, CA: McNally and Loftin, West.
1977 Farm Workers and Agri-Business in California, 1947–1960. Notre Dame, IN: Notre Dame University Press.
Garrow, David J.
1988 Bearing the Cross: Martin Luther King, Jr., and the Southern Christian Leadership Conference. New York: Vintage.
Gibney, Mark
1986 Strangers or Friends: Principles for a New Alien Admission Policy. Westport, CT: Greenwood.

Gibney, Mark, ed.
1988 Open Borders? Closed Societies? The Ethical and Political Issues. Westport, CT: Greenwood Press.
Gilad, Lisa
1990 The Northern Route: An Ethnography of Refugee Experiences. Social and Economic Studies No. 39. St. John's: Institute for Social and Economic Research, Memorial University of Newfoundland.
Gilboy, Janet
1991 Deciding Who Gets In: Decisionmaking by Immigration Inspectors. Law and Society Review 25:571–599.
1992 Penetrability of Administrative Systems: Political "Casework" and Immigration Inspectors. Law and Society Review 26:273–314.
Gilroy, Paul, and Joe Sim
1987 Law, Order, and the State of the Left. *In* Law, Order, and the Authoritarian State: Readings in Critical Criminology. Phil Scraton, ed. Pp. 71–106. Milton Keynes, UK: Open University Press.
Ginsberg, Benjamin
1986 The Captive Public: How Mass Opinion Promotes State Power. New York: Basic Books.
Goldring, Luin
1987–1990 Development and Migration: A Comparative Analysis of Two Mexican Migrant Circuits. *In* Unauthorized Migration: Addressing the Root Causes: Research Addendum, vol. 1. Commission for the Study of International Migration and Cooperative Economic Development. Pp. 381–418. Washington, DC: U.S. Government Printing Office.
1996 Blurring Borders: Constructing Transnational Community in the Process of Mexico-U.S. Migration. Research in Community Sociology 6:69–104.
Goode, Judith
1994a Encounters over the Counter: Bosses, Workers, and Customers in a Changing Shopping Strip. *In* Newcomers in the Workplace: Immigrants and the Restructuring of the U.S. Economy. Louise Lamphere, Alex Stepick, and Guillermo Grenier, eds. Pp. 251–280. Philadelphia: Temple University Press.
1994b Polishing the Rustbelt: Immigrants Enter a Restructuring Philadelphia. *In* Newcomers in the Workplace: Immigrants and the Restructuring of the U.S. Economy. Louise Lamphere, Alex Stepick, and Guillermo Grenier, eds. Pp. 199–230. Philadelphia: Temple University Press.
Gordon, Milton M.
1964 Assimilation in American Life: The Role of Race, Religion, and National Origins. New York: Oxford University Press.
Graham, Wade
1996 Masters of the Game: How the U.S. Protects the Traffic in Cheap Mexican Labor. Harpers 293(1754)July 1996:35–50.
Greenberg, James B., and Thomas K. Park
1994 Political Ecology. Journal of Political Ecology 1:1–12. http://www.library.arizona.edu/ej/jpe/volume_1/ascii-foreward.txt.
Greenhouse, Carol J.
1989 Interpreting American Litigiousness. *In* History and Power in the Study of Law: New Directions in Legal Anthropology. June Starr and Jane F. Collier, eds. Pp. 252–273. Ithaca, NY: Cornell University Press.

Grenier, Guillermo, Alex Stepick, Debbie Draznin, Aileen LaBorwit, and Steve Morris
1992 On Machines and Bureaucracy: Controlling Ethnic Interaction in Miami's Apparel and Construction Industries. *In* Structuring Diversity: Ethnographic Perspectives on the New Immigration. Louise Lamphere, ed. Pp. 65–94. Chicago: University of Chicago Press.
Griffith, David, and Ed Kissam
1995 Working Poor: Farmworkers in the United States. Philadephia: Temple University Press.
Guyot, Dorothy
1991 Policing as though People Matter. Philadelphia: Temple University Press.
Hagan, Jacqueline María
1994 Deciding to Be Legal: A Maya Community in Houston. Philadelphia: Temple University Press.
Hall, Stuart, Chas Critcher, Tony Jefferson, John Clarke, and Brian Roberts
1978 Policing the Crisis: Mugging, the State, and Law and Order. London: Macmillan.
Hammar, Tomas, and Kristof Tamas
1997 Why Do People Go or Stay? *In* International Migration, Immobility, and Development: Multidisciplinary Perspectives. Tomas Hammar, Grete Brochmann, Kristof Tamas, and Thomas Faist, eds. Pp. 1-19. Oxford, England: Berg.
Handwerker, W. Penn
1997 Universal Human Rights and the Problem of Unbounded Cultural Meanings. American Anthropologist 99:799–809.
Harwood, Edwin
1986a American Public Opinion and U.S. Immigration Policy. The Annals of the American Academy of Political and Social Science 487:201–212.
1986b In Liberty's Shadow: Illegal Aliens and Immigration Law Enforcement. Stanford, CA: Hoover Institution Press.
Hayes-Bautista, David, Werner O. Schink, and Jorge Chapa
1992 The Young Latino Population in an Aging American Society: Policy Issues Evoked by the Emergence of an Age-Stratified Society. *In* U.S.-Mexico Relations: Labor Market Interdependence. Jorge A. Bustamante, Clark W. Reynolds, and Raúl Hinojosa Ojeda, eds. Pp. 196–213. Stanford, CA: Stanford University Press.
Held, Virginia
1984 Rights and Goods: Justifying Social Action. Chicago: University of Chicago Press.
Herzfeld, Michael
1992 The Social Production of Indifference: Exploring the Symbolic Roots of Western Bureaucracy. New York: Berg.
Heyman, Josiah McC.
1991 Life and Labor on the Border: Working People of Northeastern, Sonora, Mexico 1886–1986. Tucson: University of Arizona Press.
1994 The Mexico–United States Border in Anthropology: A Critique and Reformulation. Journal of Political Ecology 1:43–65. http://www.library.arizona.edu/ej/jpe/volume_1/ascii-heyman.txt.

1995 Putting Power in the Anthropology of Bureaucracy: The Immigration and Naturalization Service at the Mexico-United States Border. Current Anthropology 36:261–287.

1998 State Effects on Labor Exploitation: The INS and Undocumented Immigrants at the Mexico-United States Border. Critique of Anthropology 18:155–179.

N.d.[a] Fieldnotes on video library of the INS Western Region, files of author.

N.d.[b] State Escalation of Force: A Vietnam/U.S.-Mexico Border Analogy. Unpublished MS.

Higham, John

1974[1955] Strangers in the Land: Patterns of American Nativism 1860–1925. New York: Atheneum.

Hoffman, Abraham

1974 Unwanted Mexican Americans in the Great Depression: Repatriation Pressures, 1929–1939. Tucson: University of Arizona Press.

Hollifield, James F.

1994 Immigrationism and Republicanism in France: The Hidden Consensus. *In* Controlling Immigration: A Global Perspective. Wayne A. Cornelius, Philip L. Martin, and James F. Hollifield, eds. Pp. 143–176. Stanford, CA: Stanford University Press.

Hondagneu-Sotelo, Pierrette

1994 Gendered Transitions: Mexican Experiences of Immigration. Berkeley and Los Angeles: University of California Press.

Horton, John

1995 The Politics of Diversity: Immigration, Resistance, and Change in Monterey Park, California. Philadelphia: Temple University Press.

Hymes, Dell, ed.

1974 Reinventing Anthropology. New York: Vintage.

Ingram, Helen, and Anne Schneider

1993 Constructing Citizenship: The Subtle Messages of Policy Design. *In* Public Policy for Democracy. Helen Ingram and Steven Rathgeb Smith, eds. Pp. 68–94. Washington, DC: The Brookings Institution.

Interpreter Releases

1990 The Immigration Act of 1990 Analyzed: Part 1—Introduction. 67(Dec. 3, 1990):1353–1358.

Jasso, Guillermina, and Mark R. Rosenzweig

1990 The New Chosen People: Immigrants in the United States. New York: Russell Sage Foundation.

Juffras, Jason

1991 Impact of the Immigration Reform and Control Act on the Immigration and Naturalization Service. The Rand Corporation Report JR-09; The Urban Institute Report 91-08. Santa Monica, CA and Washington, DC: The Rand Corporation and The Urban Institute.

Kadetsky, Elizabeth

1994 "Save Our State" Initiative: Bashing Illegals in California. The Nation 259:416–42.

Kahn, Robert S.

1996 Other People's Blood: U.S. Immigration Prisons in the Reagan Decade. Boulder, CO: Westview.

Kanstroom, Daniel
1997 Dangerous Undertones of the New Nativism: Peter Brimelow and the Decline of the West. *In* Immigrants Out! The New Nativism and the Anti-Immigrant Impulse in the United States. Juan F. Perea, ed. Pp. 300–317. New York: New York University Press.

Kearney, Michael
1991 Borders and Boundaries of State and Self at the End of Empire. Journal of Historical Sociology 4:52–74.
1986 From the Invisible Hand to Visible Feet: Anthropological Studies of Migration and Development. Annual Review of Anthropology 15:331–361.

Kinsey, Richard, John Lea, and Jock Young
1986 Losing the Fight against Crime. Oxford, UK: Basil Blackwell.

Kottak, Conrad Phillip, Jane J. White, Richard H. Furlow, and Patricia C. Rice, eds.
1997 The Teaching of Anthropology: Problems, Issues, and Decisions. Mountain View, CA: Mayfield.

Kuper, Adam
1995 Comment. Current Anthropology 36:424–426.

Kushma, John J.
1988 Participation and the Democratic Agenda: Theory and Praxis. *In* The State and Democracy: Revitalizing America's Government. Marc V. Levine, Carol MacLennan, John J. Kushma, Charles Noble, Jeff Faux, and Marcus Raskin, eds. Pp. 14–48. New York: Routledge.

Ladd, John
1975 The Ethics of Participation. Participation and Politics, Nomos XVI. J. R. Pennoch and J. W. Chapman, eds. Pp. 98–125. New York: Leiber Atherton.

Lamphere, Louise, ed.
1992 Structuring Diversity: Ethnographic Perspectives on the New Immigration. Chicago: University of Chicago Press.

Lamphere, Louise, Alex Stepick, and Guillermo Grenier, eds.
1994 Newcomers in the Workplace: Immigrants and the Restructuring of the U.S. Economy. Philadelphia: Temple University Press.

Lichtenberg, Judith
1983 Mexican Migration and U.S. Policy: A Guide for the Perplexed. *In* The Border that Joins: Mexican Migrants and U.S. Responsibility. Peter G. Brown and Henry Shue, eds. Pp. 13–30. Totowa, NJ: Rowman and Littlefield.

Lipsky, Michael
1980 Street-Level Bureaucracy: Dilemmas of the Individual in Public Services. New York: Russell Sage Foundation.

Loescher, Gil, and John A. Scanlan
1986 Calculated Kindness: Refugees and America's Half-Open Door, 1945 to the Present. New York: Free Press.

Lukes, Steven
1974 Power: A Radical View. London: Macmillan.

MacLennan, Carol
1988 The Democratic Administration of Government. *In* The State and Democracy: Revitalizing America's Government. Marc V. Levine, Carol MacLennan, John J. Kushma, Charles Noble, Jeff Faux, and Marcus Raskin, eds. Pp. 49–78. New York: Routledge.
1995 Democratic Participation: A View from Anthropology. *In* Diagnosing America: Anthropology and Public Engagement. Shepard Forman, ed. Pp. 51–74. Ann Arbor: University of Michigan Press.

Macpherson, C. B.
1962 The Political Theory of Possessive Individualism: Hobbes to Locke. Oxford: Clarendon Press.
Mahler, Sarah J.
1995 American Dreaming: Immigrant Life on the Margins. Princeton, NJ: Princeton University Press.
Marshall, T. H.
1950 Citizenship and Social Class and Other Essays. Cambridge: Cambridge University Press.
Martin, Emily
1994 Flexible Bodies: Tracking Immunity in American Culture from the Days of Polio to the Age of AIDS. Boston: Beacon Press.
Martin, Philip L.
1994 Germany: Reluctant Land of Immigration. *In* Controlling Immigration: A Global Perspective. Wayne A. Cornelius, Philip L. Martin, and James F. Hollifield, eds. Pp. 189–226. Stanford, CA: Stanford University Press.
Martínez, Oscar J.
1994 Border People: Life and Society in the U.S.-Mexico Borderlands. Tucson: University of Arizona Press.
Massey, Douglas S.
1987–1990 Economic Development and Labor Migration in Comparative Perspective. *In* Unauthorized Migration: Addressing the Root Causes: Research Addendum, vol. 2. Commission for the Study of International Migration and Cooperative Economic Development. Pp. 665–700. Washington, DC: US Government Printing Office.
Massey, Douglas S., Rafael Alarcón, Jorge Durand, and Humberto Gonzalez
1987 Return to Aztlán: The Social Process of International Migration from Western Mexico. Berkeley and Los Angeles: University of California Press.
Matthews, Roger, and Jock Young
1986 Confronting Crime. London: Sage.
Menchaca, Martha
1995 The Mexican Outsiders: A Community History of Marginalization and Discrimination in California. Austin: University of Texas Press.
Midgley, Mary
1991 The Origin of Ethics. *In* A Companion to Ethics. Peter Singer, ed. Pp. 3–13. Oxford, UK: Blackwell.
1994 The Ethical Primate: Humans, Freedom, and Morality. London: Routledge.
Migration News
1995 North America: Congress Moves on Immigration Reform: Permanent Economic/Employment. Vol. 2, No. 10. http://migration.ucdavis.edu/Archive/MN_95/oct_95-02.html.
1996 Regulating the Immigrant Labor Market. Vol. 3, No. 9. http://migration.ucdavis.edu/Archive/MN_96/sep_96-05.html.
1997a North America: INS: Management and Apprehensions; Foreign-born Population and Immigration Up. Migration News 4(5). Http://migration.ucdavis.edu/archive/mn_97/may_97-02.html.
1997b CIR Pushes for Changes. Migration News 4(12). Http://migration.ucdavis.edu/By-Month/MN-Vol-4-97/Dec.html.
Miller, Daniel
1994 Modernity: An Ethnographic Approach. Oxford, England: Berg.

Mills, Nicholaus, ed.
1994 Arguing Immigration: The Debate over the Changing Face of America. New York: Simon and Schuster.

Mines, Richard
1981 Developing a Community Tradition of Migration to the United States: A Field Study in Rural Zacatecas, Mexico, and California Settlement Areas. Monograph Series No. 3. La Jolla, CA: Center for United States-Mexican Studies, University of California, San Diego.

Nagengast, Carole, Rodolfo Stavenhagen, and Michael Kearney
1992 Human Rights and Indigenous Workers: The Mixtecs in Mexico and the United States. Current Issue Brief 4. La Jolla, CA: Center for United States–Mexican Studies, University of California, San Diego.

Newman, Katherine S.
1993 Declining Fortunes: The Withering of the American Dream. New York: Basic Books.

New York Times
1995 Buchanan: In His Own Words. December 31: A-20.

Ninivaggi, Cynthia Carter
1994 Poverty and Politics: Practice and Ideology among Small Business Owners in an Urban Enterprise Zone. *In* Newcomers in the Workplace: Immigrants and the Restructuring of the U.S. Economy. Louise Lamphere, Alex Stepick, and Guillermo Grenier, eds. Pp. 281–301. Philadelphia: Temple University Press.

Ogbu, John
1987 Variability in Minority School Performance: A Problem in Search of an Explanation. Anthropology and Education Quarterly 18:312–334.

Palerm, Juan-Vicente
1995 Policy Implications of Community Studies. Working Paper, presented at the Conference "Changing Face of Rural California," Pacific Grove, California, June 12–14.

Park, Kye-Young
1996 Use and Abuse of Race and Culture: Black-Korean Tension in America. American Anthropologist 98:492–499.

Perea, Juan F., ed.
1997a Immigrants Out! The New Nativism and the Anti-Immigrant Impulse in the United States. New York: New York University Press.

Perea, Juan F.
1997b The Statue of Liberty: Notes from Behind the Gilded Door. *In* Immigrants Out! The New Nativism and the Anti-Immigrant Impulse in the United States. Juan F. Perea, ed. Pp. 44–58. New York: New York University Press.

Pessar, Patricia
1986 The Role of Gender in Dominican Settlement in the United States. *In* Women and Change in Latin America. June Nash and Helen Safa, eds. Pp. 273–294. South Hadley, MA: Bergin and Garvey.

Petition
1992 Petition to the Inter-American Commission on Human Rights of the Organization of American States. Los Angeles: Peter A. Schey, Designated Attorney of Record.

Pigden, Charles R.
1991 Naturalism. *In* A Companion to Ethics. Peter Singer, ed. Pp. 421–431. Oxford, UK: Blackwell.
Piore, Michael J.
1979 Birds of Passage: Migrant Labor and Industrial Societies. Cambridge, UK: Cambridge University Press.
Piven, Frances Fox, and Richard A. Cloward
1977 Poor People's Movements: Why They Succeed, How They Fail. New York: Vintage.
Polanyi, Karl
1957[1944] The Great Transformation: The Political and Economic Origins of Our Time. Boston: Beacon Press.
Portes, Alejandro
1983 Of Borders and States: A Skeptical Note on the Legislative Control of Immigration. *In* America's New Immigration Law: Origins, Rationales, and Potential Consequences. Wayne A. Cornelius and Ricardo Anzaldua Montoya, eds. Pp. 17–32. Monograph Series No. 11. La Jolla, CA: Center for U.S.-Mexican Studies, University of California, San Diego.
Portes, Alejandro, and Alex Stepick
1993 City on the Edge: The Transformation of Miami. Berkeley and Los Angeles: University of California Press.
Portes, Alejandro, and John Walton
1981 Labor, Class, and the International System. New York: Academic Press.
Postel, Sandra
1994 Carrying Capacity: Earth's Bottom Line. *In* State of the World 1994. Lester R. Brown et al., eds. Pp. 3–21. New York: W. W. Norton.
Rappaport, Roy A.
1979 Adaptive Structure and Its Disorders. *In* Ecology, Meaning, and Religion. Richmond, CA: North Atlantic Books.
1993 Distinguished Lecture in General Anthropology: The Anthropology of Trouble. American Anthropologist 95:295–303.
1995 Disorders of Our Own: A Conclusion. *In* Diagnosing America: Anthropology and Public Engagement. Shepard Forman, ed. Pp. 235–294. Ann Arbor: University of Michigan Press.
Reimers, David M.
1985 Still the Golden Door: The Third World Comes to America. New York: Columbia University Press.
Repak, Terry A.
1995 Waiting on Washington: Central American Workers in the Nation's Capital. Philadelphia: Temple University Press.
Rodriguez, Néstor P.
1997 The Social Construction of the U.S.-Mexico Border. *In* Immigrants Out! The New Nativism and the Anti-Immigrant Impulse in the United States. Juan F. Perea, ed. Pp. 223–243. New York: New York University Press.
Rogers, Rosemarie
1987–1990 Return Migration, Migrants' Savings and Sending Countries' Economic Development: Lessons from Europe. *In* Unauthorized Migration: Addressing the Root Causes: Research Addendum, vol. 2. Commission for the Study of International Migration and Cooperative Economic Development. Pp. 911–936. Washington, DC: U.S. Government Printing Office

Rosenau, James N.
1990 Turbulence in World Politics: A Theory of Change and Continuity. Princeton, NJ: Princeton University Press.
Rosenau, James N., and Mary Durfee
1995 Thinking Theory Thoroughly: Coherent Approaches to an Incoherent World. Boulder, CO: Westview.
Rotella, Sebastian
1995 Smuggling Immigrants from Mexico into the U.S. Is Becoming a Booming, Sophisticated Industry. Los Angeles Times, February 5:1.
Sacks, Karen Brodkin
1994 How Did Jews Become White Folks? *In* Race. Stephen Gregory and Roger Sanjek, eds. Pp. 78–102. New Brunswick, NJ: Rutgers University Press.
Sassen, Saskia
1988 The Mobility of Labor and Capital: A Study in International Investment and Labor Flow. Cambridge: Cambridge University Press.
Scanlan, John A.
1982 Immigration Law and the Illusion of Numerical Control. University of Miami Law Review 36:819–864.
Scheper-Hughes, Nancy
1992 Death without Weeping: The Violence of Everyday Life in Brazil. Berkeley and Los Angeles: University of California Press.
1995 The Primacy of the Ethical: Propositions for a Militant Anthropology. Current Anthropology 36:409–440.
Schmitt, Eric
1997 Efforts to Reduce Legal Immigration Loses [sic] Impetus in Congress. The New York Times on the Web, January 17. Http://www.nytimes.com/1997/Jan/17/.
Schurmann, Franz
1974 The Logic of World Power: An Inquiry into the Origins, Currents, and Contradictions of World Politics. New York: Pantheon.
Selby, Henry A., Arthur D. Murphy, and Stephen A. Lorenzen
1990 The Mexican Urban Household: Organizing for Self-Defense. Austin: University of Texas Press.
The Select Commission on Immigration Control and Reform
1981 U.S. Immigration Policy and the National Interest. Washington, DC: U.S. Government Printing Office.
Shannon, Margaret
1990 Building Trust: The Formation of a Social Contract. *In* Community and Forestry: Continuities in the Sociology of Natural Resources. Robert G. Lee, Donald R. Field, and William R. Burch Jr., eds. Pp. 229–240. Boulder, CO: Westview.
Sheridan, Thomas E.
1986 Los Tucsonenses: The Mexican Community in Tucson, 1854–1941. Tucson: University of Arizona Press.
1995 Arizona: The Political Ecology of a Desert State. Journal of Political Ecology 2:41–57. Http://www/library.arizona.edu/ej/jpe/volume_2/ascii-sheridan.txt.
Silberbauer, George
1991 Ethics in Small-Scale Societies. *In* A Companion to Ethics. Peter Singer, ed. Pp. 14–28. Oxford, UK: Blackwell.

Simon, Rita J., and Susan H. Alexander
1993 The Ambivalent Welcome: Print Media, Public Opinion, and Immigration. Westport, CT: Praeger.

Singer, Audrey, and Douglas S. Massey
1997 The Social Process of Undocumented Border Crossing. Paper presented at the meetings of the Latin American Studies Association, Guadalajara, Mexico.

Stapelton, Seton
1991 Immigrant Visa Availability under the Immigration Act of 1990: Initial Observations from the Visa Office. Interpreter Releases 68(April 1):373–383.

Stefancic, Jean
1997 Funding the Nativist Agenda. *In* Immigrants Out! The New Nativism and the Anti-Immigrant Impulse in the United States. Juan F. Perea, ed. Pp. 119–135. New York: New York University Press.

Stehr, Nico
1996 The Salt of Social Science. Sociological Research Online 1(1). http://www.socresonline.org.uk/socresonline/1/1/1.html.

Stolcke, Verena
1995 Talking Culture: New Boundaries, New Rhetorics of Exclusion in Europe. Current Anthropology 36:1–24.

Stull, Donald D., Michael J. Broadway, and Ken C. Erickson
1992 The Price of a Good Steak: Beef Packing and Its Consequences for Garden City, Kansas. *In* Structuring Diversity: Ethnographic Perspectives on the New Immigration. Louise Lamphere, ed. Pp. 35–64. Chicago: University of Chicago Press.

Stull, Donald D., Michael J. Broadway, and David Griffith, eds.
1995 Any Way You Cut It: Meat Processing and Small-Town America. Lawrence, KS: University Press of Kansas.

Stull, Donald D., and Jean J. Schensul, eds.
1987 Collaborative Research and Social Change: Applied Anthropology in Action. Boulder, CO: Westview.

Swartz, Marc J., Victor W. Turner, and Arthur Tuden
1966 Introduction. *In* Political Anthropology. Marc J. Swartz, Victor W. Turner, and Arthur Tuden, eds. Pp. 1–41. Chicago: Aldine.

Taylor, Ian
1981 Law and Order: Arguments for Socialism. London: Macmillan.

Turner, Bryan S.
1986 Citizenship and Capitalism: The Debate over Reformism. London: Allen and Unwin.
1990 Outline of a Theory of Citizenship. Sociology 24:189–217.

Uphoff, Norman
1996 Learning from Gal Oya: Possibilities for Participatory Development and Post-Newtonian Social Science. London: Intermediate Technology Publications.

U.S. Commission on Immigration Reform
1989 Statistical Yearbook of the Immigration and Naturalization Service. Washington, DC: U.S. Government Printing Office.
1994 U.S. Immigration Policy: Restoring Credibility. Washington, DC: U.S. Government Printing Office.

Van Willigen, John
1993 Applied Anthropology: An Introduction, Rev. edition. Westport, CT: Bergin and Garvey.
Vélez-Ibañez, Carlos
1996 Border Visions: Mexican Cultures of the Southwest United States. Tucson: University of Arizona Press.
Waal, Frans de
1996 Good Natured: The Origins of Right and Wrong in Humans and Other Animals. Cambridge, MA: Harvard University Press.
Walzer, Michael
1983 Spheres of Justice: A Defense of Pluralism and Equality. New York: Basic Books.
Whelan, Frederick G.
1988 Citizenship and Freedom of Movement: An Open Admission Policy? *In* Open Borders? Closed Societies? The Ethical and Political Issues. Mark Gibney, ed. Pp. 3–39. Westport, CT: Greenwood Press.
Wolf, Eric R.
1969 Peasant Wars of the Twentieth Century. New York: Harper and Row.
1974a[1964] Anthropology. New York: W.W. Norton.
1974b[1969] American Anthropologists and American Society. *In* Reinventing Anthropology. Dell Hymes, ed. Pp. 251–263. New York: Vintage.
1982 Europe and the People without History. Berkeley and Los Angeles: University of California Press.
Woodrow, Karen A., and Jeffrey S. Passel
1990 Post-IRCA Undocumented Immigration to the United States: An Assessment Based on the June 1988 CPS. *In* Undocumented Migration to the United States: IRCA and the Experience of the 1980s. Frank D. Bean, Barry Edmonston, and Jeffrey S. Passel, eds. Pp. 33–75. Santa Monica, CA and Washington, DC: Rand Corporation and The Urban Institute.
Yelvington, Kevin
1995 Producing Power: Ethnicity, Gender, and Class in a Caribbean Workplace. Philadelphia: Temple University Press.
Yelvington, Kevin, ed.
1993 Trinidad Ethnicity. Knoxville: University of Tennessee Press.
Zavella, Patricia
1997 The Tables Are Turned: Immigration, Poverty, and Social Conflict in California Communities. *In* Immigrants Out! The New Nativism and the Anti-Immigrant Impulse in the United States. Juan F. Perea, ed. Pp. 136–161. New York: New York University Press.